V∎ETNAM WARHORSE

A HUEY PILOT'S MEMOIRS

VOLUME 1

VIETNAM WARHORSE

A HUEY PILOT'S MEMOIRS

VOLUME 1

TOLD BY A TWO-TOUR US ARMY IROQUOIS ('HUEY') PILOT
DURING THE VIETNAM WAR. A TRIBUTE TO THE MANY
WHO FLEW THIS WONDERFUL WARHORSE.

RICHARD GUAY

VIETNAM WARHORSE: A HUEY PILOT'S MEMOIRS VOLUME 1
Copyright © 2024 by RICHARD R. GUAY.

Printed in the United States of America.

For more information, or to book an event, contact :
Website: https://richardguayauthor.com
Email: https://admin@richardguayauthor.com

Book design by Richell Balansag & Heru Setiawan
Cover design by Jude Mag-asin

ISBN - Paperback: 978-1-7635948-0-7
ISBN - Hardcover : 978-1-7635948-1-4
ISBN - Ebook: 978-1-7635948-2-1
ISBN - Audiobook: 978-1-7635948-3-8

First Edition: 2024

CONTENTS

PART ONE
BASIC TRAINING

PART TWO
FLIGHT TRAINING

PART THREE

FOREWORD

Lt. General Sylvester

What a great read!

If you ever served in the military, went through boot camp or basic, and especially if you ever went to flight training—and ultimately anyone who ever went to war—read this book!

I know I laughed, might have even stifled a tear or two, but what I did most was remember. Not only did this kindle memories in my consciousness, it awakened a synapse or two that took me back to some days that were worth reinstating firmly in my brain housing group!

This Yank, now Aussie, has a style distinctly with an American bent, but laces in some Aussie humor and perhaps a bit of Irish too! This great American served with distinction, as did his father, and you can see he has "been there and done that . . . even got a T-shirt!" Now he writes to inform, to please, and most especially to revive the memories of the many thousands of the rest of us who shared his experiences.

John B Sylvester
Lieutenant General, US Army, Retired

Authors Note: Brian Wizard is the author of *"Permission to Kill"* which is based on his time served as a door gunner on a Huey smokeship during the Viet Nam War... His website is **https://bwizard.art/**

Richard Guay's book *Vietnam Warhorse: A Huey Pilots Memoirs* is versatile and caters to various reading preferences. Whether you're into campfire storytelling, bedtime reading, or even reading during your commute or on the toilet, this book is for you. It offers compelling anecdotes about his engagement in the Viet Nam War as a Huey helicopter pilot, providing a taste of war for readers who have not experienced it firsthand. The book also delves into the finer details of military training and hands-on combat, making it comprehensive.

Short stories follow Mr. Guay's military training and combat tour, each succinctly capturing its title's essence. These anecdotes not only provide a taste of the helicopter war in Viet Nam but also offer profound learning, developed expertise, and personal enhancement. If you're seeking a book that is easy to read, without the need to retain the details of where you left off, this beauty is for you.

Enjoy,

Brian Wizard

With this book, you accompany Richard through several chapters of his life's journey. You get one man's view of US Army basic training with many of its funny events. You get a first-hand view of becoming a US Army helicopter pilot going through flight training and even getting lessons on helicopter aerodynamics and emergency procedures. He is one of some 41,000 pilots who went through helicopter training at Ft Wolters, TX during the Vietnam era (I am one also).

You get to see how he taught himself early in his career to fly to the edge of the flight envelope to gain valuable knowledge of flying helicopters. There are two kinds of pilots: the "early dreamers", those who at a young age dream of flying, and the "late deciders", those who decide to become a pilot as a profession later in life. Richard is one of those "early dreamers" and pursued his dream to become a pilot.

After completing flight school, he takes on the journey of flying to Vietnam and becoming a helicopter co-pilot and later an Aircraft Commander in the Vietnam War. As a "slick" or "Huey" pilot he shows how he received on-the-job training in the art of a helicopter war.

He gives you insight into some serious, some tragic, and some funny war stories as "you are there" with him. His stories will spark similar memories in any Vietnam veteran helicopter pilot myself included.

You can watch his progress from flying "slicks" (troop transport) to "guns" (gunship helicopters) as he proved his knowledge, experience, and superb airmanship abilities. His combat missions were first to move American troops and then later protect them. In war, lifelong "comrades in arms" are developed and a unique" brotherhood" is nurtured. Richard gives you an insider's view of that brotherhood. I look forward to reading Richard's future books of more of the chapters in his life.

Reviewer – Walter Sipes, PhD, Tucson, AZ.
282nd Assault Helicopter Company, HHC, 212th Combat
Aviation Battalion 1970-71 Marble Mountain, Da Nang, RVN
Clinical Psychologist in the US Air Force for 16
years, NASA psychologist for 15 years.
Currently, an Aerospace Psychology Consultant supporting
Axiom Commercial Space and Canadian Space Agency.

REVIEW ON
VIETNAM WARHORSE:
A HUEY PILOT'S MEMOIRS

BY

RICHARD GUAY

What a brilliant book! A very personal story of one man and his flying machine... at war!

No ordinary man and no ordinary machine - the Huey helicopter - the 'Warhorse' of the Vietnam war. A Warhorse which went *above and beyond* in multiple ways.

The Huey had a huge impact on troops both 'friendlies' and the 'enemy' throughout the long Vietnam war, more so than any other aircraft in any war before or since.

This is the story of the magnificent flying machine but equally importantly it is the story of a man who piloted the Huey all over the world and that story is very personal. It is well worth reading!

The book is an honest account of a man 'at war and at peace'. It records the very active life of Richard Guay, someone I have known for over 50 years, someone who until now has kept many of his exploits private.

Richard is not a braggard and his writing style reflects that, it is *not* a 'look at me' book. He is a down-to-earth guy who anyone would love to have as a friend and he has shared many of his experiences in bite sized chapters.

The details Richard provides the *Dear Reader* (as he refers to us) are at times gripping, exciting, funny, frank and sometimes raw, always vivid, always informative and always interesting. For some readers it will bring back memories, for others it may reinforce an inner need to get 'out there' and fly.

Regardless, whether you are someone who aspires to fly, a qualified aviator, or someone who simply loves a great story this is the book to read - you will not be disappointed!

W N N Forbes
Lt Col (Retd)
Australian Regular Army
(2Lt - Platoon Commander Vietnam 1972-73)

ACKNOWLEDGEMENTS

This book could not have been written without the support, encouragement, editing skills, and steadfastness of Ms. Maria Collins, to whom I shall always remain indebted. I owe my thanks and sincere gratitude to my former roommate, Patrick Mullen, Spartan 12, while we served with the 190th Assault Helicopter Company, Bien Hoa, 1969 and 1970. Patrick's library of photographs and video footage is amazing, and I shall always remain truly thankful for his carte blanche permission for my use of them. The faultless illustrations by Katherine Nielsen portrayed beyond description where words failed. 'The Angel of Can Tho' is a classic example. The advice and technical assistance I received from Margaret Hiatt was timely and thorough. I owe a debt of gratitude to all of those who have permitted me to use their photos, diagrams, names, etc., in this publication. I would not have written this book without selfpublishing.com. Their professionalism and mentoring in every step of the writing and production of this book are world-class. I thank Chandler Bolt and his entire crew for their incredible assistance.

My deepest thanks to publishers David and Charles (Publishers) Ltd. for granting permission for the use of this wonderful book, considered the go-to publication for helicopter general knowledge to those of my generation and beyond. Please refer to the following:

Author: John Fay
Title: *The Helicopter: History, Piloting, and How it Flies* by John Fay, 1954, 1967, 1976
Illustrated by Lucy Raymond, David Gibbings, and Dulcie Legg
Published by David and Charles (Publishers) Limited
Davidandcharles.com

PREFACE

I wrote this book for several reasons. My main motivation was to encourage those who have always wanted to fly to take the next step into the utter freedom one feels while soaring through a blazing blue universe, to experience the exhilaration of flight, the feeling of purpose, and the wonderful sense of achievement on a daily basis. If this is you, this book may encourage you to take the necessary steps toward becoming a professional pilot. I believe there is currently a huge demand in the rotary wing profession for more pilots. Those of us who flew in Vietnam have now retired, and I suspect the vacuum created is larger than the potential supply required to fly helicopters almost anywhere in the world.

I have done my best to take the mystery out of military communications and use the basic English language. I've composed my memoirs in short story form, so the book can be put down wherever you choose without worrying about plots, subplots, counterplots, et cetera. All of the incidents are as true to life as I can remember them.

Of course, there is always the motivation of entertainment. Otherwise, why would anyone read someone else's experiences? I truly hope that you enjoy the humor, the heartache, and the experiences of an intense wartime environment. I have chosen to include information about the dynamics of flight, sometimes even explaining what is going on in the mind of the pilot, as if you were sitting right next to him during critical maneuvers—which instruments to observe, what tolerances can't be exceeded, how all of those gazillion moving parts work together to defeat gravity by staying aloft to 'get the job done!'

I've included a few stories about basic training, the officer and flight training of a warrant officer candidate, and gone to great lengths to include a wide range of tasks performed while flying the venerable UH-1 Iroquois (Huey) helicopter in various combat scenarios.

If you would like, click on the QR code below, and you can watch my interview with the Library of Congress, which was made into a documentary to be archived indefinitely as part of the history of the Vietnam War. Keep in mind there is no audio for about the first minute.

MEET YOUR AUTHOR

QR Code Library of Congress Documentary, Vietnam Veteran, Richard Guay

URL: https://youtube.com/watch?v=GV1vvwdJSbc

The URL below will take you to the official website of the 190th Assault Helicopter Company, please have a look and add human faces to this book, not necessarily by name, but a general wander through the living history portrayed in the book.

https://190thahc.com/

A PROLOGUE

THE SIGNING OF THE PARIS PEACE ACCORDS AND THE PEACE TREATY BETWEEN EGYPT AND ISRAEL

The Paris Peace Accords were signed on January 27, 1973, between the United States, the Democratic Government of Vietnam (North Vietnam), the Republic of Vietnam (South Vietnam), and the Provisional Revolutionary Government of the Republic of South Vietnam (PRG), which represented the South Vietnamese Communists. This treaty no doubt saved many lives in this terrible conflict.

The negotiations for this document covered a three-year period, during which time my biological father, United States Air Force (USAF) Brigadier General Georges R. Guay, was the USAF Air Attaché to France. Col. Guay, as he was known during this period, was the principal negotiator on behalf of the United States government, answering directly to President Nixon and the US National Security Advisor Henry Kissinger. Col. Guay and Le Duc Tho, who represented the interests of North Vietnam, met many times in Paris.

As the agreement was drafted, one section at a time, Dr. Kissinger would travel to Paris and sign the current section. These many meetings eventually culminated in the final document, the Paris Peace

Accords. Col. Guay told me himself that, with the signing ceremony at hand, Dr. Kissinger asked him what he wanted for his efforts. Dad's reply was, "Just a seat at the table for the signing."

Within a few months of the Paris Peace Accords being signed, Col. Guay was assigned as Defense and Air Attaché to Egypt, working from the US Embassy in Cairo. He intended to contribute to the facilitating of a peace agreement between Egypt and Israel. Over some time, he and Anwar Sadat, the then-president of Egypt, became close friends. My father believed that during this extended time, and considering this friendship, he did, in fact, further the eventual signing of the peace treaty between Egypt and Israel following the 1978 Camp David Accords. This treaty still stands to this day. He told me that when Anwar Sadat was assassinated, it broke his heart.

Brigadier General Guay refused to write a book about his part in saving many lives. He once told me he wanted no personal recognition for his participation in these monumental peace declarations. For this reason, I have included this prologue in my book, in honor of the incredible service he performed for his country. In my opinion, he was a giant of a man.

B.G. Georges R Guay

<u>United States Air Force Brigadier General</u>
<u>Georges R. Guay (Deceased)</u>

A STATEMENT REGARDING THE HISTORICAL
CONTEXT OF THE CONTENTS OF THIS BOOK

I have written this book with its text coinciding with the period of history in which it is contained. It reflects society's views at the time and may contain religious, gender, racial, or sexual and other language that may be offensive by today's standards. The views represented by any third party do not necessarily represent the views of the author, including via URL, or QR Code, except for the QR code linked to The Library of Congress Interview of the Author.

PART ONE

BASIC TRAINING

Richard Guay with his M-14 rifle.

1

ARRIVAL AT FORT POLK, LOUISIANA, FOR BASIC TRAINING

I t was a lovely spring day in June 1968. As I arrived at the appointed time and place in downtown New Orleans to board the bus that would take me to Fort Polk, Louisiana, I did not realize I was beginning an entirely new life. I was very excited to be joining the Army, my blood pressure surely running high. Standing in the group of about forty fellas, I suspect we all had the same basic emotions: apprehension, excitement, dread, and joy. I believed this day was predestined and unavoidable, yet exciting. As I imagined what would happen, I realized the one thing working for me was that I was a military brat. I had a general knowledge of the attitude of those in charge, some idea of how I was about to be treated, and knew there would be no escape.

The bus trip seemed to take forever. There was the usual amount of excited chatter, but my anticipation sharpened with every mile that passed. Even the trip to clear the New Orleans city traffic seemed to take forever. Once we hit Interstate 10 and reached seventy miles an hour, I relaxed a bit and began to notice the people around me. The cross-section of humanity aboard the bus was amazing.

There was almost every nationality you could think of. Every color of skin, length of hair, you name it. The draft had been going full speed then. I suspect it had snared most of those aboard in its net; however, I had volunteered. Later, while going through basic training, I learned that volunteering for service would be a distinct advantage. Having 'RA' (Regular Army) in front of my service number every time I shouted it out to get into the mess hall elicited smiles from the drill sergeants. RA stood for the Regular Army, those of us who enlisted. 'US' was the term used by draftees to refer to the fact they were drafted. They would get harassed at almost every stage as they went into the mess hall. This could amount to anything from a bit of hazing to being sent to the back of the line.

The bus arrived at Fort Polk around 2:00 p.m. As it pulled to a stop, the door opened, and we disembarked, carrying our few belongings with us. We were immediately herded into a rectangular formation by four drill sergeants, who screamed randomly at us the whole time. As I was trying to elbow my way into this formation, one of the drill sergeants stopped immediately in front of me, his face directly in front of mine.

"What the hell do you think you are doing, maggot?" I was ready for this, but not for the volume or the fact that he was spitting in my face while shouting.

I stammered some weak explanation. Once again, he shouted at the top of his voice, "Do you like me, maggot?"

"Umm, er, yeah, sure," was the only thing I could think to say.

"Oh, you like me, do you? Well, likn' leads to lovin', and lovin' leads to fuckin'! Do you want to fuck me, maggot?"

My immediate reply came easily, "No, drill sergeant!"

"You don't want to fuck me? Whassa matter, ain't I good enough for you?"

At this, I had to smile. I looked him right in the eye, a slight smile projected with the corners of my mouth.

Then he screamed at the top of his lungs, "Get out of my face and go stand over there!"

I truly believe that is the last thing in the world he expected to see from someone who should have been shaking in their boots. As I mentioned, sometimes, being a military brat paid off.

To start, they stripped away our individuality with a GI haircut and gave us everything needed for basic training. We were briefed on the Uniform Code of Military Justice, mess hall routines, and the Army's conduct and moral expectations. As things settled down, a rhythmic routine became the order of the day. In the beginning, the drill field became a well-known piece of real estate. Every time someone did something wrong or out of sequence, he was immediately ordered to do fifty push-ups.

The drill sergeant woke us up every morning at 0500 hrs. (using the twenty-four-hour clock, 1:00 p.m. became 1300 hours, or hrs., and so forth) by banging a steel garbage can and yelling for us to get up and fall in by 0530. We held our platoon formation in front of our barracks, giving the drill sergeant plenty of time to scrutinize us useless maggots. Looking back, it's interesting how well we all got to know each other during our eight weeks crammed together in almost every stressful situation imaginable.

There were many written rules we had to follow, and then there were a few unwritten rules that we adhered to in the natural order of things. Showering every night, wearing clean clothes every morning, and shaving in the morning as opposed to the evening were some unwritten rules. This brings to mind one of the funniest stories I can recall.

Our platoon was made up entirely of trainees for warrant officer candidates, which we learned in the first week of basic training. Of course, at that stage, none of us had any idea that was the case. However, a drill sergeant from another platoon let the cat out of the bag, resulting in many discussions about our prior aviation experience. It turned out that one of our platoon members had been an airline pilot. Without the benefit of a university education, the only way he could fly was to join the Army and become a warrant officer pilot. Of course, this was the same for all of us. However, he was probably twenty-five or-six, and with our average age of nineteen, it almost made him seem like an old man.

He was always big-noting himself as a 'Don Juan' with the ladies. The typical tall, handsome, blue-eyed boy. Really, he was setting himself up for a fall by constantly bragging about his conquests. During week four, someone noticed he had started shaving at night. This is what we called a *Romper Room* no-no, a phrase taken from a child's television program that inferred something like a mortal sin. The dictum of standardization required all of us to do the same thing at the same time. No one should be able to 'change the system' to their benefit.

An unknown person conveyed to our platoon sergeant that this individual was shaving at night. The next morning, after we had our platoon inspection, we changed into our PT uniforms and went to the physical training field for our usual routine.

As we arrived, Sgt. Giesler gave the command, "Dress right, dress!"

This was a standard inspection formation with plenty of room between each soldier, and definitely a surprise. He left us at attention and inspected each of us with a hard stare. Sgt. Giesler stopped in front of our airline pilot and peered up at his chin from his 'lofty' height of five-three. The airline pilot was about six-three, so there was plenty of room for our favorite sergeant to take a good gander.

"Maggot, did you shave this morning or last night?"

We all listened intently, knowing life would rapidly worsen if he lied.

"I shaved this morning, drill sergeant."

"Is that right?" queried Sgt. Giesler. "Well, I have it on good authority that you, in fact, shaved last night. Before you answer this next question, I suggest you consider your answer carefully. If you lie, you will live to regret it. Now, did you shave last night or this morning?"

Our airline pilot hesitated. I suspect he knew the jig was up. "I shaved last night, drill sergeant," he replied.

"So, you lied to me?" There was a pregnant pause. "Maggot, go to your foot locker and bring back your steel pot and your razor."

Without saying another word, the airline pilot took off at the double to fetch the items requested. Upon his return, he handed said items to the drill sergeant.

"Maggot, can you sing?" asked Sgt. Giesler without the hint of a smile.

"No, drill sergeant, I cannot sing a note," came the reply.

Without another word, Sgt. Giesler handed the airline pilot his steel pot.

Please keep in mind that this is the helmet worn in all those World War II movies. It was made of molded steel and was heavy and quite large.

When worn, it was suspended on top of a tortoiseshell liner, which differs from modern helmets. The comfortable liner had light canvas webbing to protect the head and a chinstrap. We only wore the heavy steel pots when we were in dangerous situations. When worn correctly, the tortoiseshell and steel pot combination can protect the wearer from shrapnel. Without the tortoiseshell, the steel pot will rest on top of someone's head, with the bottom edge of the pot at about chin height. Wearing a steel pot without its liner is impractical and comical, causing it to wobble and slip off.

Sgt. Giesler instructed our airline pilot to place the steel pot upon his head without its liner. "Now, jump up and down on one leg," he commanded.

Upon doing so, it made a sound quite like a loud bell ringing.

Oh boy! I bet that hurts! I was thinking.

The sergeant then handed the individual his double-edged razor blade. The poor bastard was then told to sing "The Star-Spangled Banner." Once this concert in motion was established, with the steel pot banging around on his head while he hopped up and down on one leg and sang "The Star-Spangled Banner," Sgt. Giesler suddenly shouted, "Now shave!"

Holy shit, this was one of the funniest things I had seen at this point in my life! This entire scenario seemed unbelievable.

As this ridiculously funny scenario played out, not one person in the formation laughed out loud. We knew if we had done so, we would be joining that poor, arrogant soul in his actions. Trust me, this made a totally new man out of our arrogant airline pilot. He became very sociable and reasonably humble, and his face healed nicely over time.

2

CLEANLINESS IS NEXT
TO GODLINESS

If someone passed the draft physical, a reasonably stringent examination of every cavity and extremity of one's person, they could be reasonably assured that they would receive a letter from 'The Draft Department' of the United States Government congratulating them on being selected to serve their country in a time of war, in whatever capacity said government had chosen for them. However, should we choose to volunteer, we were guaranteed the Military Occupational Specialty (MOS) we selected. Hence, those of us that chose to be helicopter pilots were volunteers. Collectively, we all knew the job would be dangerous, but my fellow recruits and I didn't see it as a problem.

During my time in the military, I developed an experience-based theory: "There is always the 10 percent who refuse to perform or behave as expected or required." In this case, I'm talking about those who don't match our idea of how a soldier should look or act.

Our basic training company was Echo Company, 5th Battalion, 1st Training Brigade, or in our vernacular, "E-5-1." They billeted our eighty-man platoon in the old WWII, two-story timber buildings, which were common at Fort Polk (or Fort Puke, as we used to call it).

I mention this because we had a majority of budding pilots in our platoon, meaning we had to meet additional requirements, such as body mass, height, et cetera, with the residual being draftees of every size and description. The one person that stood out in the mix of all platoon members was a morbidly obese young man, Maggot Henry. He was a real 'piece of work.'

I suspect that from the day he arrived at Fort Puke, the world was not a happy place for Maggot Henry. He was about six feet tall and weighed nearly 320 pounds. He wore a permanent sneer on his face, and his shoulders drooped terribly as he walked.

Henry was not good at anything. Every morning before breakfast, we would all run one mile, but not Henry. We jogged in formation, and the weaker ones fell to the rear. The fear of punishment caused people to lend a hand to those who had difficulty finishing the run. The only problem was we all knew, after about the second run, that Henry would be last.

After about the fifth day of jogging, the drill sergeant saw the futility of anyone hanging back and trying to help Henry. He weighed a ton, didn't try very hard, and couldn't give a damn whether or not he finished the run. Eventually, he was allowed to walk. I'm sure he thought that was fine because all we had to do was run an *extra* mile before breakfast. There were repercussions for this in the making, I assure you.

Another one of Henry's terrible traits was not showering—ever. After about a week, the fellas near Henry's bunk had a powwow. That evening, there was a lot of yelling and stomping around as they went down the stairs to the latrine area. After you walk through the open area of the nine-toilet latrine, you make your way to the shower block. This is where a now-naked Henry found himself with four other nude men and a huge, very stiff laundry scrubbing brush. No one was in a kind mood or cared what Henry thought about this. It was time for him to get clean. And boy, oh boy, did he get clean!

He screamed as if he were falling from a mile-high cliff. When he came out of there, his entire body was cherry red, and he was extremely angry. He tried taking a few pokes at some fellas, very much to his regret. After they landed a few good punches on him, he decided to calm down.

Henry's ultimate mistake in judgment of the entire platoon played out at the low crawl pit—four large rectangular areas with four-by-fifty-feet-long shallow ditches dug the entire length of the rectangle. Each ditch was about three feet wide. About twelve inches above the bottom of these little ditches was a crisscross woven spiderweb of sharp barbed wire. The ditches were at least six inches deep in mud, not a nice place to be. Following the instructions from our drill sergeants, we all fell into our alphabetically formed lines, determined by our surnames, which became automatic after a while.

A drill sergeant at the beginning of each row of four pits watched us launch into the mud and keep our butts and heads down, avoiding the overhead wire. Once we got to the other end of the pit, saturated with thick, black mud, we returned to the starting point, getting back into line to repeat the process, four times in total.

Well, Henry had other ideas. When it was his turn, he flopped down on his stomach and virtually had to flatten out like a viper. I'm sure he found this exceedingly difficult and most upsetting. Indeed, he would have been nicked in his butt and back more than once by barbed wire.

He low crawled on his fat belly to the other end of the pit, with a drill sergeant walking beside him, screaming at the top of his voice the whole time, "You fat-ass slug, you piece of whale shit, you are a lazy, slimy, filthy, fat afterthought. Move your big fat ass and keep it down. Otherwise, I will kick the wire into your big stinking butt!"

Eventually, Henry made it. He was utterly exhausted and filthy.

Immediately upon Henry exiting the lane, the drill sergeant quickly returned to the start point for that group of pits. However, Henry strolled to the starting end of the pit, then continued walking on past it. Just before he could make a clean break in whatever direction he had chosen, our drill sergeant captured him and returned him to our platoon.

The drill sergeant reached the end of our particular ditch and stopped all the other maggots from entering. Sgt. Giesler spoke loudly to the platoon once the trainees had left the pits and returned to the traffic jam at the start point of each lane.

"This maggot"—he had Henry standing beside him now—"has decided, in his wisdom, that he would only have to do the low crawl once, while you are doing it four times."

Immediately, we all started looking at each other, waiting for Sgt. Giesler to drop a bomb. It didn't take long! "Therefore, you will all do one extra lap in the low crawl pit! This dumb, fat grub doesn't have to do anything. He will stand with me and watch your sorry filthy asses do the extra lap."

A thousand daggers were stared into Henry's head! The hatred was palpable while we stood there, shifting from foot to foot at the head of the low crawl pits.

"All right, you bunch of pukes, line up and get going!"

And so we did, a grand total of five laps of the low crawl pit. Every pair of eyes were riveted on Henry as we began our extra lap.

After completing our five laps in the pit, we marched back to our barracks, showered, changed uniforms, and went to the mess hall. There were a lot of low-volume discussions among the tables; trouble was afoot for Henry. Then we marched back to the barracks and began our evening routine of tidying everything up, getting it ready for the next morning's inspection. Hardly a word was spoken among the troops, but the die had been cast.

Fireguards were posted on each floor from lights out until 0530. Lights out was at 2100 hrs., and the usual quiet prevailed. At 2130 hrs., there was movement everywhere, but it was silent. There were forty bunks on our floor and forty on the upstairs floor. The occupants of the first floor were busy preparing their socks, inserting a fresh bar of soap down into the toe. I was terribly conflicted in my thoughts. *Is this the right thing to do?* I knew he wouldn't be 'wounded,' only hurt. However, we had done everything we possibly could to cajole him, without any success. So yes, we collectively needed to make a point, and he would hopefully respond by showing some effort to 'become one of us.' Oh dear, were we ever wrong.

By now, Henry was sound asleep. Someone instructed the fellow from the bunk bed above Henry to fold his towel into a narrow strip. Henry was already lying flat on his back, making it easy to throw the towel across Henry's eyes as his bunkmate leaned over the victim's head from the outside end, pressing hard and pinning him down on the bunk while everyone lined up.

In turn, one by one, we hit Henry with our soap bar in a sock, swinging it at whatever speed our emotions prescribed, in an orderly manner. Some of us swung it once; others swung it twice or even three times. One good whack on the belly with the prescribed device made me feel much better, even though I could feel a sense of discord within my conscience about what was happening. While all of this pummeling was going on, each of us whispered something in Henry's shell-pink ear. Some called him names, and some gave advice. I whispered, "Get your shit together." We got back in our bunks, leaving Henry in a fetal position, moaning and groaning.

The following day, Henry's walk resembled the shuffle of a ninety-year-old man. Our platoon sergeant called for us to fall in and watched Henry as he took his place in the formation.

Sgt. Giesler marched straight to the first maggot in the front row and, in a booming voice, asked, "What in the hell is wrong with that big, fat fucking maggot over there?" while pointing at Henry.

"He fell down the stairs, drill sergeant!" The individual replied in the same volume as the question was asked.

We all had hoped that this terrible lesson would have resulted in an attitude of readjustment in Henry's head. As it turned out, there was nothing of the kind. Two days later, Henry went AWOL (Absent Without Leave). During a time of war, this is a severe charge. When we learned what Henry had done, none of us gave a damn. We just shrugged our shoulders, rolled our eyes, and got on with the job.

However, the saga does not end here. Three days later, lo and behold, there was Henry, back in formation when we fell in for our morning inspection. Later that morning, the entire platoon was lined up to receive our required five injections for being shipped out to Vietnam. As luck would have it, Henry was standing in front of me while we were taking two or three steps at a time. Sgt. Giesler and two medics, one on each side of the line, were jamming needles into our arms or firing a smooth-faced air-powered gun that injected the serum into our arms where the needles usually went.

Just as Henry was stepping up to this team of medics, the drill sergeant that marched us into this rather painful situation said quietly to the medics, "This goddamned maggot went AWOL two nights ago." He said it with a smile, which surprised me.

Then I knew why: the two medics injected Henry simultaneously. One said, "He's not getting away with that!"

As Henry walked away to form up for the march back to the barracks, he still had a needle hanging out of each arm, gently flopping up and down as he walked.

As a result of his behavior during the entire eight weeks of basic training, the ultimate punishment was issued for Henry. He was recycled and had to do the entire eight weeks again. I don't think we ever discovered what happened to Henry, nor did we care.

'Baseball' hand grenade.
Photo supplied by Patrick Mullen, Spartan 12, Stogie 13.

3

THE HAND GRENADE RANGE

As with all armed forces, the US Army left nothing to chance when it came to training inductees in the use of lethal force. We were continually marched from one classroom to another, resulting in a reasonably good education regarding the use of whatever weapon system we were learning. This was usually done on a daily basis. In my opinion, one of the more exciting ways of blowing things up was with hand grenades. Our initial training in the use of hand grenades entailed a reasonable march to the hand grenade range.

Upon arrival, we were broken into sections of twelve. We were then handed practice grenades, the same shape and weight as a live grenade, containing a 'live' fuse but no explosive charge. This was to get the feel of what it was like to throw one, followed by a little 'pop' made by the blasting cap when the real explosion would have occurred. We were then marched into rather long trenches. This is where we would initially stand to throw our inert hand grenades, with the target being another trench quite a distance away. There was a wire stretched between the two trenches about twenty-five feet high, and we were told if we could throw the hand grenade over the wire, we should reach the other trench where the hand grenade would explode, with the small 'pop' still audible.

Our section began tossing these simulated grenades. On my second throw, I actually managed to get my grenade into the opposite trench. It helped to have played shortstop in Little League. All that practice finally paid off. However, I had to be told of my success in reaching the opposite trench, because once we threw the grenade while shouting, "Grenade!" we had to drop to the bottom of the pit, in case the weapon went off while airborne, and killed us with its imaginary shrapnel.

After finishing the exercise in the trenches, we were again all lined up and handed another practice grenade, which we were then instructed to throw through a window in the mock-up house approximately fifty feet away. To the best of my memory, I don't think anyone got the grenade through the window. We truly had no measure of the weight of this lump of metal compared to a baseball.

The construction of the M-67 fragmentation grenade is remarkably simple. The fuse is a device consisting of a lever, which is called a spoon, and the retaining pin, which is called the pin. The pin must be pulled out, allowing the spoon to release the striker and ignite the grenade's fuse, causing it to explode. The fuse is similar to a dynamite blasting cap. Approximately two-and-a-half inches long, round, shiny silver-colored tube, only about three-eighths of an inch wide, and filled with gunpowder.

This fuse/pin assembly fits directly into the center of the grenade (and the plastic explosive pack). The entire mechanism is screwed into the center of the body. After the spoon is released, with a four- to five-and-a-half-second delay, it explodes and sets off the entire charge, resulting in the release of the fragmented case plus thousands of small pieces of shrapnel from a wound piece of wire, nicked at close intervals, which will break apart upon detonation of the charge.

I might add that the ease with which the fusing system can be unscrewed, then tossed only a few feet away and fired with a quiet 'pop,' then reassembled so that the grenade looks totally unaltered, was a constant source of mirth when used to play jokes on the unsuspecting!

From time to time, several platoons would be combined for live-fire training exercises. It so happened that the grenade practice range and the grenade live-fire range were large enough to accommodate two platoons simultaneously. Whenever these exercises were initiated, and our sister platoon was included in the exercises, we always looked forward to seeing 'Barry!'

Barry was a unique individual. He was about five-six, with rather large eyes and a constantly excited expression on his face. Nowadays we would know him to be hyperactive, but I don't know if that diagnosis existed back then. Whenever Barry would stop to speak to someone, his feet would keep going, up and down, up and down, up and down, up and down. He was always running in place. His face was alive with enthusiasm, and his arms were always kind of pumping. I think the only time Barry may have held still was when he was sitting down in a classroom. He always did his best to conform, but the problem was you never really *knew* what he was actually going to *do*! With Barry in mind, please allow me to describe how the 'live-fire' grenade range worked.

The layout of the live-fire range, where we threw armed grenades, was quite simple. Each pit was roughly six feet across and about eight feet deep, surrounded all the way around by a one-foot-thick concrete blast wall. In the center of the pit was a round hole, into which the training sergeant would kick a live grenade in case it was dropped. The internal design of the hole would then contain the explosion and shrapnel.

Throwing pits were entered from the rear. Should this be the first throw for the trainee, the grenade would still be contained in its small, sturdy paper tube. The training sergeant would instruct the trainee to remove the grenade from its tube, place the tube into a disposal container, and hold the grenade as trained in the classroom, with the spoon under the thumb of his throwing hand.

Training sergeants would then look the trainee in the eye, size him up, and ask if he was comfortable with what he was about to do. Most of us were excited; we couldn't wait to hurl this instrument of death and destruction at a car tire down range and blow it to pieces!

Personally, when asked, I nodded in the affirmative. Actually, I never heard of anyone not wanting to throw a grenade—it was just too damned exciting.

"Pull pin." Upon this command, we were instructed to turn sideways to the direction of the throw, hold the grenade in front of our chests, with our elbows diametrically opposed, and pull the pin. Now we had a live, extremely dangerous object in our hands. The training sergeant was watching our every move like a hawk.

"Throw!" was the next command. Each of us threw the bastard as far as we could from our position, while yelling at the top of our lungs, "GRENADE!" Alerting all others that you had just unleashed all hell and fury at your target 'down range' and in front of you . . . what could possibly go wrong? There were at least ten of these pits, side by side in a row, all connected to each other by a mutual blast wall in a straight line.

Then it was Barry's turn. I got this story from one of the guys in my platoon, who was the next in line behind him. Oh dear!

We had to carry the device in both hands, one on top, one on bottom, with elbows diametrically opposed, facing each other. When Barry was handed the grenade in its paper tube, he carried it in the prescribed fashion, but his feet started going up and down, like the cylinders in a Chevy 427 cu. in. V-8 engine, while he waited his turn to enter the throwing pit.

Upon entering the pit, the brave training sergeant looked him up and down and yelled, "Goddammit! Hold still!"

Barry suddenly realized his feet belonged to him, and he stopped the pumping in place.

"Remove the grenade," came the next command.

Without a problem, Barry twisted the two halves, opened the tube, and placed the paper tube into the disposal container. Apparently, his eyes were as big as saucers.

"Are you okay with this?" came the mandatory question.

Barry started pumping his feet again and quickly nodded yes.

"Maggot! Hold your feet still!" came the next command.

Once again, Barry stopped running in place, still holding the grenade with both hands in the prescribed fashion.

The training sergeant was really looking at him hard by this stage. I suspect he was wondering if he was going to survive the next two moves.

"Pull pin!"

With this command, Barry, being left-handed, placed the grenade in his left hand, thumb over the spoon, with elbows flat, and directly in front of him. He inserted his right index finger into the pull ring, holding the grenade in his left hand, then he pulled the pin, just as instructed. The following command was a real corker.

"Throw!" the training sergeant shouted in a firm, authoritative voice.

Now let me explain. Barry was in pit number one, on the left end of the ten pits. Of course, each pit was numbered in order. Barry turned sideways and threw the grenade as hard as he could—except he held on to it too long and used the sidearm throw, as it was called in baseball. Both Barry and the sergeant yelled, "Grenade!" as the little bomb flew across pits two, three, four, and five, and they kept yelling, "Grenade," as did the other nine persons throwing their grenades. Pit six, still airborne, seven, eight, watch it, now arcing down! Nine, and finally landing about one foot in front of—but safely down range from—the protective blast wall in pit number ten!

Apparently, the training sergeant in pit ten glimpsed the grenade landing directly in front of his blast wall and was able to drag his hapless maggot down to the ground just as the weapon of small destruction exploded with an ear-shattering concussion. Blast force and shrapnel slammed into the foot-thick concrete wall less than two feet in front of them, luckily allowing them to avoid all of the paperwork that would have accompanied maiming and possible death!

Probably for the first time in his life, Barry's training sergeant was speechless. He stood there panting, then finally composed himself and looked Barry straight in the eye. And Barry? Fuck! His eyes were bugging out of his head. His feet were hammering in place, arms pumping, an expression of amazement on his face.

"Get the fuck out of my pit! Right now!!" came the command.

Barry looked down the line and could see the occupants of pit number ten standing up, so he knew they were okay. With that, he turned around, virtually marched out through the rear entrance, and joined the others waiting behind the pits. So ended another experience in the daily life of one of our brothers, Barry.

4

THE SPIRIT OF THE BAYONET

Bayonet for M-14 rifle. Illustration by Katherine Nielsen.

Excerpt from: War Department 7 September 1943
WAR DEPARTMENT BASIC FIELD MANUAL
FM 23-25
BAYONET
SECTION 1
GENERAL

1. *THE SPIRIT OF THE BAYONET: The will to meet and destroy the enemy in hand-to-hand combat is the spirit of the bayonet. It springs from the fighter's confidence, courage, and grim determination, and is the result of vigorous training. Through training, the fighting instinct of the individual soldier is developed to the highest point. The will to use the bayonet first appears in the trainee when he begins to handle it with facility, and increases as his confidence grows. The full*

development of his physical prowess and complete confidence in his weapon culminates in the final expression of the spirit of the bayonet—fierce and ruthless destruction of the enemy. For the enemy, demoralizing fear of the bayonet is added to the destructive power of every bomb, shell, bullet, and grenade which supports and precedes the bayonet attack.

2. *USES OF THE BAYONET: a. A determined enemy may not be driven from his position by fire alone. Making full use of cover and concealment, he will often remain in his position until driven out in hand-to-hand combat. The bayonet or the threat of it, therefore, is the ultimate factor in every assault.*

    b. At night, on infiltration missions, or wherever secrecy must be preserved, the bayonet is the weapon of silence and surprise.

    c. In close combat, when friend and foe are too closely intermingled to prevent the use of bullets or grenades, the bayonet is the primary weapon of the infantry soldier.

As I get older, I think about how the US Army trains ordinary people to kill. When the draft was in full swing, most of these young men would have been straight out of high school. However, it doesn't really matter what their age might have been. Over eight weeks of basic training, the bayonet course gradually helped us develop the right mindset to accomplish such a goal.

I have always wanted to share this opinion with anyone who would listen. The intensity of emotion that was conjured in one's psyche during these few hours of training was truly amazing. The bayonet course was a tremendous step toward turning ordinary civilians into true warriors, more so than just firing a rifle.

Allow me to explain the process involved in dehumanizing your brother or the guy across the street.

I recall already feeling empowered and competent in handling the M-14 rifle, the ultimate mounting point for the bayonet. The morning they issued us our bayonets, there was a bit of a buzz in the air once we had the sheathed blade strapped onto our pistol belts.

There is something very primal about envisaging stabbing another human. I suppose this goes back to cave dweller days.

We were told this was going to be a company-sized exercise, meaning there would be over 300 of us taking part at the same time. We picked up our M-14s, fell into formation, and marched with the rest of our company of approximately 320 men. It was not a long march, and we arrived at an enormous field with a tall square platform, approximately six feet high by six feet square in its center. Large outdoor speakers stood on each corner of the platform, each on their own eight-foot-tall mount. Standing in the center of this platform was a drill sergeant, representing the epitome of a warrior of the United States Army. He was about six-four, dark-haired, and muscular in his freshly starched fatigues. The golden eagle on his flat-brimmed drill instructor's hat shone brightly, and he held a microphone in his hand.

Each platoon drill sergeant positioned his platoon opposite another to form a square with the platform in the center. Then, they gave a command, causing the forty men of each platoon to form a straight line. This resulted in an almost closed square formation around the senior drill sergeant in the center of the formation.

Using the PA system, the senior drill sergeant instructed the company to stand at ease and spoke about the bayonet. The essence of his message was strictly in line with the *War Department Field Manual 23–25, The Spirit of The Bayonet,* mentioned above. His only interruption during the droning presentation taken from said field manual was to give the command, "Company! Double time, march!" Thanks to our training, over 300 maggots instantly began jogging, resulting in a circle with the large platform immediately in the center, the troops about twenty yards out from the middle.

"Unsheathe bayonets!" came the command through the loudspeakers. While jogging comfortably in a circle, we unsnapped the handles of our bayonets and took them out of their sheaths.

"Hold them over your heads! Now, as you have been instructed, what is the spirit of the bayonet?"

"To kill!" we shouted.

"What is the spirit of the bayonet?"

"To kill," we all yelled in unison.

"What is the spirit of the bayonet?" he bellowed into the sound system.

"To kill!" we were all screaming now.

"I can't hear you!"

"To kill!" we yelled at the top of our lungs.

"I still can't hear you! Sound off like you've got a pair!"

"To kill!" we screamed once more.

Again, he yelled into his microphone, "What is the spirit of the bayonet? What is the spirit of the bayonet?!"

"To kill, to kill, to kill!"

There we were, about 320 soon-to-be warriors double-timing in a large circle, screaming our heads off, "To kill, to kill, to kill!" We had been worked into an absolute lather. By now, the adrenaline was roaring through our veins. Caught up in the moment, we started waving our razor-sharp bayonets over our heads, stabbing the air. "To kill, to kill, to kill, to kill!"

I believe this is when the US Army instilled the killer instinct into our psyche. Pardon the pun, but it really was a double-edged goal. We learned how to kill, and to defend ourselves simultaneously, making us less sensitive to violence. The point of this training seems to be forgotten. *Any form of combat* is a two-sided coin. Honest to God, in any scenario, combat comes down to a simple adage, 'kill or be killed.'

We spent the rest of that day learning how to 'fix bayonets' or, in plain English, how to attach and remove the bayonet to and from the end of our rifles. We practiced running at our imaginary foe and screaming as we stabbed these fixed bayonets into straw bales with each corner roped to large black timber posts. Before removing the bayonet, they taught us to twist the rifle to avoid the difficulty caused by a vacuum created by the blood encasing the blade, making it almost impossible to withdraw the impaled blade from a body.

We learned the following movements using the rifle with a fixed bayonet: whirl, long thrust, short thrust, withdrawal, parry right and left, vertical and horizontal rifle butt strokes, including smash and slash. These were the grist for the mill for someone who depended upon one knife attached to the end of his weapon in a battle to the death. I still think of that full-length scar on Sgt. Giesler's back, from top right to bottom left, and what a horrible fight he must have had to win.

Additionally, we learned how to sneak up from behind, hold our enemy's mouth shut, and either stab him in the kidney or slit his throat for a swift death. *We became desensitized regarding attacking and killing another human.* As the sun set, we felt incredibly excited and exhausted.

The withdrawal from adrenaline feels like your muscles are burning, and ours were on fire, but our lives now had a view through the keyhole of 'kill or be killed.'

After our basic training final graduation parade, Sgt. Giesler told us we were real soldiers now with a stripe on our sleeves and had done a great job as a basic training platoon. All of us progressing to flight training packed our duffel bags and boarded the bus to Fort Wolters, Texas, the initial destination for every US Army helicopter pilot.

Now, let's leave the basic training behind, and start talking about one of the real joys of life—flying.

PART TWO

FLIGHT TRAINING

5

HELPFUL TRAITS OF
MOST PILOTS

What I am going to share with you now is my experience-based advice. It is not from a textbook; it is what I have been able to glean from over thirty years of experience flying helicopters. This also includes over 3,000 hours of flying time in a two-person cockpit. I can assure you that thousands of helicopter pilots worldwide have the same knowledge as I do—and, in many cases, infinitely more—but haven't taken the time to put it into a book.

I want to make it perfectly clear that what I am saying in this chapter is *not required* to make a pilot. Please don't be discouraged if you feel you may not 'measure up' or feel confident enough to continue because those of us who want to fly, I believe, are born that way. From the age of four, I wanted to be a pilot. At that age, I used to hammer sticks together with nails in the backyard and throw whatever contraption I invented through the air as far as I could, hoping it would fly.

My feelings never changed from that age until now. All I can say is that for the areas I'm about to cover, it would behoove you, as a potential aviator (if you're not already a qualified flier), to pay particular attention. They certainly helped me during a rather long career in aviation.

Whether or not you are still in some form of dedicated education—high school, university, etc.—you must be prepared to study very hard when it comes to learning the laws of physics related to the joy of flying. I realize that's a very broad statement. However, it starts with the basics, such as the aerodynamic traits of aircraft design. I could fill up several pages just discussing aircraft lift. The main thing is this all goes back to the time we spent—mostly in high school and university—studying such things as mathematics, physics, chemistry, and perhaps basic engineering. Please don't throw this book up in the air and walk away. I guarantee it won't fly!

Speaking as the former manager of a helicopter flight school, the academic line of delineation between success and failure to pass the academic subjects necessary to attain a commercial pilot license was a minimum of grade ten education. Once most of you have that level of education, I believe you could be on your way.

In rotary-wing aircraft, if you felt a vibration develop, sometimes you would have less than a minute to figure out where it was coming from before you had to decide what to do with the aircraft (basic engineering). In other words, will it have a potentially catastrophic result if you continue to fly? Or perhaps simply by changing throttle settings, you would be able to isolate the vibration to either the tail rotor or main rotor. I will say I never had to land because of the vibration developed in flight. I only ever had to nurse the aircraft home again if the vibration was severe enough.

After flying helicopters for approximately twenty years in the varying terrain of swamps and marshes, to the 14,000-foot mountains of Papua New Guinea, just north of Australia, we had a standing joke among the pilots I knew. "You have to be half crazy to want to fly a helicopter!" In a way, this was true. To be a successful pilot, you need to have a sense of adventure, along with a great deal of advanced knowledge of rotary wing flight and basic aeronautical knowledge. I'm not saying that one needs to be a swashbuckler, like a pirate crew in the *Pirates of the Caribbean* movie series with Johnny Depp.

Still, a sense of adventure was most rewarding when you could see what you were doing was rather rare, and afforded you great satisfaction when the day's work was done. Undoubtedly, any of you who have witnessed videos of helicopter rescue, or resupply, et cetera, would have no trouble understanding my former statement.

When I think back to times during my US Army flight training, I realize the importance of *curiosity*. Our initial training started at Fort Wolters, Texas. Our schedule involved flying in the morning and class in the afternoon, or class in the morning and flying in the afternoon. This exposed us to various types of weather.

I mention this because it was fascinating learning our subject matter in the classroom at various stages of our training. We were given a helicopter and flying solo after a lesson on who knows what. Holy smoke, what an incredible opportunity to experiment! I remember attending a morning class and learning about vortex ring state, or another name more commonly used, settling with power.

Simply put, should you inadvertently put yourself into a scenario of low airspeed while descending, say landing a helicopter in a no-wind condition or tailwind, or hovering at an altitude higher than that used to taxi from A to B on a tarmac, with the wind coming from behind the aircraft (tailwind), you are guaranteed to crash if you have insufficient altitude to recover from this maneuver. There has certainly been more than one helicopter photography session ending in disaster because of this scenario.

In class, we were told that if we slowed our airspeed to the point of losing our translational lift, which is required to maintain a state of flight, by perhaps hovering at altitude with the wind coming from the wrong direction, then no matter how hard we pull the collective control upward, which should result in the aircraft climbing, without performing a certain recovery maneuver, we were doomed to fail because the helicopter would be descending into its own downward wind, or rotor wash. Consequently, this scenario would only increase your rate of descent all the way to the point of impact on Mother Earth. Well, there was one sure-fire way of testing that theory!

At this time, I might add that studying math, science, and physics in high school is one of the best ways to familiarize yourself with the aerodynamics of flying a helicopter. All principles of flight, from the most basic concept to space travel, are based on Newton's laws. The more familiar you are with the in-depth study of physics, the easier it is to understand the workings of a helicopter. As I've heard many times, "A helicopter does not fly. It beats the air into submission." If you have a broad-based general knowledge of physics, you can understand why this statement and its accompanying humor are true.

In my next solo flight session, after performing the perfunctory pre-flight checks and accomplishing the takeoff, I immediately started climbing and, at the same time, tracking away from the main airfield. By the time I reached 6,000 feet of altitude, I was well and truly out over the desert. I guided the aircraft away from the airfield, which was now approximately seven miles away, and began decreasing my power while bringing the chopper's nose upward, slowing my airspeed. Being a fledgling pilot, I wasn't quite sure of the wind direction, so I increased my engine power while holding the nose higher until the aircraft began to shake almost violently, and I began to descend rapidly through the downward motion of my rotor wash. The more I increased the upward pitch in the main rotor and should have been climbing, the faster I hurtled toward the earth!

I had successfully initiated the maneuver called vortex ring state or settling with power. I could see the earth rushing up to meet me at a very rapid rate. All the little dots in the desert were becoming relatively more significant bits of vegetation. The horizon seemed to be rushing at me as my field of vision was filling with the light cream color of the desert floor, replacing almost all of the sky's blue! When I realized the speed at which I was descending, my heart started racing, and I experienced a massive surge of adrenaline. That was really scary!

Remember, I started this experimental flight over a mile high. Of course, I had memorized the procedure for recovery and had spent quite a bit of time learning this critical procedure by the numbers: 1) I lowered the collective pitch all the way down, 2) maintained flight rpm (revolutions per minute) on the main rotor, 3) moved the cyclic control to full forward position (the cyclic control dictates the tilt of the main rotor) and then 4) slowly increased my manifold pressure (the amount of power from my engine that was being delivered to the main rotor) until I was at hover power. This is a higher power setting than what is necessary to fly the helicopter straight and level. The vibrations started to smooth out, and I began to fly forward out of the massive vertical momentum I had established.

I began to relax as I could feel the aircraft moving forward, and checked the airspeed indicator to see that I had picked up about thirty knots of airspeed in forward flight, and confirmed my recovery by looking at the altimeter, which indicated I was leveling off. I then pulled the collective control up to the maximum allowable engine power setting and commenced to climb again while maintaining flight rpm for the main rotor.

Looking at the altimeter, I realized the aircraft was just under 3,000 feet of altitude. I had lost over 3,000 feet of height in less than a minute and was quite astounded, to say the least. I knew I would never again perform that maneuver without much planning beforehand. I also knew exactly what to look for should I ever get into that scenario accidentally.

In my career as a civilian commercial helicopter pilot, this never happened again. I knew how to say, "No," when some photographer wanted a particular photo in 'this' direction out 'this' door, which might result in us going into settling with power (usually because we would have been trying to hover at altitude in a tailwind). Unfortunately, many new, inexperienced commercial helicopter pilots don't have the courage to tell a client no and explain that it is for the safety of them both, that perhaps they could do the flight in a different direction and photograph from another door.

As a point of interest, once I became a UH-1 'Huey' Instructor Pilot while in the First Cavalry Division at Fort Hood, Texas, each check ride I gave, I demonstrated settling with power. Many of my students, who had a minimum of one tour in Vietnam and consequently over 1,000 hours of flight experience, had never experienced it before. They were quite surprised by the severity of the maneuver and how quickly it could be overcome using the prescribed procedure, resulting in a safe recovery.

One of the innate traits every good aviator should have is a *sense of caution*. When I say this, considering my former statements in this chapter, I do not mean 'overcaution.' We all need to have that little man on our shoulder that most of us never listen to. We are either about to do something foolish, or we've already done it, and now we have got to find our way out of it before the laws of physics choose to make us pay the price. I suppose I'm saying that once you start using your imagination to consider various scenarios you think you may enjoy, make sure you think them all the way through to the conclusion.

Additionally, a great sense of humor is one of the best personality traits I can think of for pilots, and all of us throughout life in our chosen endeavors. Our lives would be extremely stressful if we didn't have a sense of humor. Imagine going through life being upset by one incident or another and then stewing over it for the rest of your life or for months on end—this will only result in unhappiness that will more likely make you ill.

Those of us who may choose to aviate are required to keep a cool, logical mindset. I can guarantee you that part of a good demeanor on a busy day will require a solid sense of humor. Very often, small incidents, perhaps in inefficiency or procedure at some stage, or somebody just 'doing the wrong damn thing,' need to be laughed at, not sworn at. I firmly believe that stress is cumulative during a day's activity while you're in charge of a helicopter. Unscheduled and unexpected occurrences can happen, and the results must be lived with. In my opinion, being able to laugh off such a situation will certainly increase your life span.

Remember, when you feel your muscles tightening up because something upsets you, as one other pilot once told me, take three deep, relaxed breaths. You will be amazed at how much this helps you calm down.

There will be situations while you're flying where life truly does imitate art. Honestly, your life can sometimes be like a movie— sometimes a good movie, sometimes a bad movie. Rudyard Kipling composed a poem that captures the subject. Here is an excerpt:

"If—"

If you can keep your head when all about you
Are losing theirs and blaming it on you;
If you can trust yourself when all men doubt you,
But make allowance for their doubting too;
If you can wait and not be tired by waiting,
Or being lied about, don't deal in lies, . . .

Yours is the Earth and everything that's in it,
And—which is more—you'll be a Man, my son!

Think about it. As illustrated in the above poem, you do not have the luxury of losing your head, having panic attacks, or any other form of loss of mental control. None of these are beneficial to someone responsible for making almost instantaneous decisions. Okay, one more quick story.

The weather that day was a clear blue sky, but the wind was gusting up to thirty knots. I was one of a team of two helicopter pilots. The owner of the small helicopter company had asked us to do joyrides from a pad on the immense Yarra River snaking its way through Melbourne, Australia.

It was March 1988, the time of Moomba celebrations, and there was an air of excitement around the vast city. The other pilot for the day had passed his commercial pilot helicopter license check ride the day before. Hence, his grand helicopter flying experience totaled 130 hours of flight time. Considering the windy conditions, I told him I thought I should fly that day, and he could do the admin work in the small office next to the Yarra River helipad. Of course, he was disappointed. However, he understood that the blustery weather wasn't exactly ideal for a newly licensed pilot.

No sooner had we opened the small office than a father and his eleven-year-old son appeared before the bench. I couldn't tell who was more excited, but the father explained that it was his son's birthday, and he had promised him a ride in a helicopter. After parting with his hard-earned cash, Dad and his son followed me to the Kawasaki

KH-4 helicopter. I did a quick walk around with them, showing them the essential bits and bobs that made the helicopter fly. Then I got them into the cabin and strapped them in. You could see the degree of high expectation on the boy's face.

I settled into my seat, strapped in, started the aircraft, made the necessary radio calls, and we were off. Our route took us from the Yarra River pad over the Melbourne Cricket Ground. Then, with a right turn, we were to fly over the Elizabeth Gardens and make another right turn toward the docks of St. Kilda, and the final leg, another right turn for the approach to land on the Yarra River pad.

Just before reaching my cruising altitude of 1,500 feet, the aircraft was struck with an updraft so violent that even though I maintained my grip on the control, the collective slammed to the full down position, but we were still shooting upward for about another thirty feet. I stabilized the aircraft and commenced the right turn when suddenly, with no warning or explanation, the helicopter flipped upside down!

All my years of training immediately kicked in, but nothing seemed to work correctly. I distinctly remember looking up through the roof of the canopy at the Yarra River while spinning slowly. I immediately tried to figure out if I should crack the door open on the way down so that when we hit the water, it might be possible to open the doors and exit the aircraft. By this time, I had done one full 360-degree rotation around the mast of the chopper.

"Mayday, Mayday, Mayday!" I called on the Essendon Tower frequency. I had made up my mind long ago that I would never die alone, and the radio was my only source of sharing my last moments with the world. "Kilo Hotel Sierra is upside down going into the Yarra adjacent to the MCG"—Melbourne Cricket Ground—"Mayday, Mayday, Mayday!"

I put the collective down, flattening the pitch in the main rotor. I then retarded the throttle to flight idle as if I were in autorotation and pushed the cyclic around in a full 360-degree circle, trying to analyze whether or not I had a break in the linkage to the swashplate, which controls the angle of attack of the main rotors. Nothing worked, so I pulled the cyclic control into my stomach, not knowing what else to do.

In retrospect, one phenomenon I was experiencing, which I had heard about but had no idea was true, was that my brain had gone into time dilation—slo-mo.

My senses were super acute. It was like watching something in slow motion. This visual phenomenon roared through my brain, and I was processing my thoughts at the same speed. As I commenced the second inverted rotation, still looking through the top of the bubble, these last words went through my mind, *So these are the jaws of death!* Really? How corny can one get? I assure you my entire life didn't flash before my eyes. I was too damn busy trying to control the situation.

Because I was in total sensory overload, I somehow thought I had experienced an engine failure. About the time this thought struck me, and I suppose only because I had pulled the cyclic control back into my gut, the nose of the aircraft started to roll from its inverted configuration into a vertical dive. Acting purely on instinct, I began to level my flight path. When I saw that I had complete control of the flight controls, and not seeing anywhere to land, I instantly picked a tall dead tree, with its branches like many arms extending upward, to land in from my autorotation.

The maneuver I thought I would have to execute, because I still had no engine power and could not reach any open area, was one often discussed among pilots in Vietnam as we were constantly flying over jungle.

I lined the aircraft up so that I could perform a rapid cyclic climb over the top of the tree, pointing the nose at the sky and 'pogo' in backward, tail rotor first, into the arms of the waiting branches, rather than land in a deep river and be locked in by water pressure on the large doors, which I was sure we would be unable to open.

While these thoughts were going through my mind and I was about to pull back into that cyclic climb over the tree, I looked at the tachometer and saw that my engine was still running.

I yelled into the radio, "I've got power! I've got power!"

So, I immediately increased my engine speed to flight rpm and continued leveling my flight path and flying the aircraft, and selected an open picnic area among the trees in the Elizabeth Gardens adjacent the Yarra. At this stage, I began to initiate a controlled landing straight into that area, which was extremely tight. I remember seeing families randomly scattered around the area having picnics. I'm sure they got quite a surprise!

As I brought the aircraft to a hover, I had an overwhelming sense of confusion. However, I wasn't on the ground yet. As I lowered the aircraft onto its skids, I automatically started the engine shutdown procedure.

Suddenly, the father, sitting in the back seat, banged me on the shoulder and said, "That was fantastic! Son, did you hear that? That was a real Mayday call!"

Christ! I almost had a heart attack! I had completely forgotten that I had passengers! Exactly at this point, I went into shock. All of my actions were now on autopilot. It seemed as though blood was draining from my head, and my brain seemed to shut down for a few seconds.

I don't recall very much of anything from this point onward until a park ranger came to my open door, and asked, "Mate, would you like a cup of tea?"

I will share with you that right now, in my office, with the door closed, I am having a quiet cry. Post-traumatic stress disorder (PTSD) is a real bastard. Reliving that near-death experience has opened a box I have managed to keep closed for a very long time.

The next day, I worked with the owner of the helicopter to perform what amounted to a forensic examination of the series of events. All control linkages were checked, potential overspeeds were investigated, and nothing pointed to a control linkage problem. I thought the main rotor gearbox clutch had failed, which would have caused the main rotor to spin uncontrollably. It wasn't that. Thinking of scenarios that would explain what happened proved futile.

About six weeks later, Ray, the owner of the company, had a firsthand experience with similar turbulence in a fixed-wing aircraft.

They were on short final, landing at Essendon Airport when they were hit by a downdraft so severe that as he was holding on to the aircraft's dashboard cover with both hands, he completely ripped the cover off, thus exposing all the wiring and instrument connections below it! After discussing this, we agreed I had been hit by a microburst.

Remember, we had thirty- to forty-knot wind gusts that day. Melbourne is a large city full of very high multi-story buildings. We believed I had entered the vortex of a small, inverted tornado called a microburst.

The rotors did not fold around the helicopter while I was inverted because the relative wind surrounding the aircraft was traveling downward at the same speed that the helicopter was falling. Once the aircraft fell out of the upside-down tornado and assumed a vertical dive flight profile, and because I had the cyclic control pulled fully aft, then, as with any aircraft, when the helicopter entered undisturbed air, I pulled out of my dive and was immediately able to resume controlled flight, leveling the chopper, and avoiding the unthinkable.

At that time, the Commonwealth Aviation Safety Authority (CASA) published a monthly flight safety magazine. I sent them a short story based on the above experience. However, in their wisdom, they did not print it. I would genuinely love to hear the tapes that were made of my calls to Essendon Tower while all of this was going on. What an eye-opener that would be.

I have shared the above story with you intending to prove something I had just previously mentioned. As a pilot, we do not have the luxury of losing control of our thoughts and the processes they create when one is confronted with an in-flight emergency.

Imagine if I had just thrown my hands up and started praying while looking through the top of the canopy and spinning around. My passengers and I would have become a statistic. As a footnote to the story, the mother of that family of three rang my cell phone the next day.

"Are you the pilot of the helicopter that my husband and son flew in yesterday?"

"Yes," I replied, giving her my name.

She then gave me her name and said, "Thank you for saving my husband and son. He only just realized everything that happened last night."

To tell the truth, I cannot remember my reply. At the time, I was pushing a shopping trolley in a supermarket, and when she hung up, I drove it into a corner, then stood there and cried my eyes out, sobbing, totally out of control.

I was with my partner at the time, and her doctor's office was at the same shopping center. After I regained my composure, we went to his office, and he saw me immediately. He explained that I was experiencing post-traumatic stress disorder, and it would 'go away in a few days.'

Well, in one sense, he was right. I did 'calm down' in a few days. However, during those few days, I think my mind was building a box to put those emotions into and put a firm bow around the whole experience.

6

THE BEGINNING OF FLIGHT TRAINING ARRIVAL AT FORT WOLTERS, TEXAS

A sign beside the main highway said, "Fort Wolters," and as the bus turned in that direction, we were full of piss and vinegar. We were beginning a pilgrimage to a destination that, for many, would affect the rest of our lives.

Going through the gates at Fort Wolters was a significant moment that brought many physical and emotional challenges.

The bus pulled up to our new two-story, concrete, freshly painted barracks, and came to a halt. That's when the shit really hit the fan! There is only one way to describe what happened when the door to the bus opened, absolute chaos!

A black helmeted, sun-glassed, highly decorated Chief Warrant Officer

Warrant Officer Candidate Richard Guay.
Fort Wolters, Texas.

Locker display: note open security locker above hats.

2 helicopter pilot, which we were to call a TAC officer (TAC stood for training, advising, and counseling), was there to make one thing clear.

"Get off my bus right now!" He kept screaming that mantra as he ran up and down the aisle of the bus, smashing the handrails with some kind of short stick. "Get out, get out, get out, now, now, now, move, move, move!"

I can tell you we weren't smiling anymore. The psychological impact of this entrance was like being slapped extremely hard in the face. "Get off my bus now! Pick up your duffel bags! Fall in!" He seemed to be looking for a fifty-man-platoon-type formation. Fall in? Where? We were scrambling like a bunch of lemmings looking for a cliff.

When we finally squeezed through the door and emerged onto the dirt, we found that the bus driver had already raised the baggage doors along the length of the bottom of the bus. Each bay was stuffed with stacks of green duffel bags containing our worldly possessions. Each bag was stenciled with names and serial numbers belonging to the occupants, loaded randomly.

Oh, by the way, there were three more of these black-helmeted demons running among the several buses, all screaming, "Grab your bags! Fall in!" No matter how many times we were told to 'fall in!' we still didn't know where to go!

Suddenly, our prayers were answered. A TAC officer was seen standing in front of the edge of a white-painted brick retaining wall. The western sun shone on his black helmet, and his sunglasses reflected our terrified faces. He remained expressionless, while the swarm of screaming devils was still running and stomping among this gaggle of maggots, harassing them in any way they could think of.

"What the hell is your name? Your name has too many letters. How do you say it? If you're mine, I'm gonna call you alphabet!"

This was all going on while I was frantically searching for my duffel bag. With all the cargo doors open now, the bus looked like a silver-and-green-striped caterpillar. The first arrivals were rifling through the bags and throwing them all over the place while searching for their own.

The next thing I knew, I heard this screaming in my right ear, "You're too goddamn slow, do you hear me?!"

I straightened up, looked at this male version of a banshee straight into his sunglasses, and said, "Yes, sir."

"Stop beady-eying me! Eyes straight ahead! Yes, sir! That is *not* how you will address your TAC officer! You will say the following, 'Sir, Candidate Dipstick, yes, sir!'"

By now, my ears were absolutely ringing! He continued, "How do you say your stupid name? It has too many vowels in it!"

"Sir, Candidate Guay!" I said, pronouncing it 'gay.'

"Okay, Candidate Guay, go fall in with that gaggle in front of that TAC officer up by the wall."

He was pointing to the lone TAC officer who had his back to the barracks retaining wall, quietly observing this Chinese fire drill of motion. It was only then that I noticed each of the TAC officers had a clipboard.

The lone senior TAC then called out, "Listen up!"

Suddenly, all the screaming stopped, and all eyes locked on to the speaker. As he said this, the other four TAC officers started lining up abreast, some distance apart.

"When you hear your name called, fall in on the TAC officer that calls it out."

The individual TAC officers then began calling out names, and we fell in line with each officer, consequently forming what was to be our permanent platoon assignment.

They assigned this new warrant officer candidate to Flight Alpha One (A-1) of the First Warrant Officer Candidate (WOC) Company, or in US Army shorthand, 1st WOC. Our TAC officer was CW2 Donald Frye, his nickname, 'The Bear.' I'm sure it was because he looked like one.

Each warrant officer candidate company had its own color, and the 1st WOC was red—hence, we were the 'Big Red One.' These three words were belted out at the top of our lungs each time the company was called to attention by each of the four platoons of fifty men. We did it in the mornings or after a fire drill. Shouting, "BIG RED

ONE!" four times in succession at 0300 hrs. and waking all persons in earshot was not appreciated by the other nine WOC companies.

HELL WEEK

At the beginning of our officer training, the TAC officers were everywhere, like a rash! During room assignment, meeting your new roommate, learning how to operate a monstrous floor polisher and how to display your uniforms, socks, and jocks (underwear)—everything that was anything in our new world. And all the while they were yelling and screaming in your face.

"When you see a TAC officer approaching you in the hallway, you will brace! That means, six feet before he reaches you, you will slam your back, your ass, and your heels flat against the wall, assume the position of attention, and shout the greeting of the day, 'Sir, Candidate so-and-so, good morning, sir!' With your eyes straight ahead, and don't you dare beady-eye me!"

'Beady-eye' meant looking straight into the officer's eyes, as in conversation. By God, they meant what they said!

A beady-eye usually resulted in fifty push-ups. When talking to a TAC, we were to stand at attention, look straight ahead, and speak clearly to avoid being singled out for mistakes.

The next four weeks placed all of us in an unbearable pressure cooker. Every morning, we held our company formation. The company commander would make any announcement about the proposed day. When finished with the day's business, he would always ask loudly, "Who wants to quit?"

The first time I heard this, I was appalled. Suddenly, when you looked around, you would see hands in the air. I couldn't believe it. These were the men who, for whatever reason, wanted out of the program. I couldn't comprehend the squandering of such an incredible opportunity. But I was learning not everyone thought like me.

The program had destined these 'quitters' for Vietnam as either door gunners or infantry. This asking about quitting continued for at least another three weeks, with more than a few soldiers opting out. I suspect that the amount of harassment and required discipline was just too much for many of them.

PRE-FLIGHT

The remaining three weeks after Hell Week were called 'pre-flight.' This was the beginning of our classroom instruction and learning of all the other daily routines. We would 'form up' into platoon formations and march daily to our classes. I think we all enjoyed our marching songs, which were many and varied. We marched to classes in platoon formation while our candidate sergeant sang marching songs and gave commands.

It was the beginning of a Texas winter, clear and snappy cold. One of the first marching songs we learned went like this: "I don't know, but I've been told. Eskimo pussy is mighty cold!" They taught us another marching song that went like this: "I don't know, but I believe," and the formation repeated it, "I don't know, but I believe, I'll be home by Christmas Eve!" These little ditties lifted our morale, and we enjoyed them.

The education we received at Fort Wolters was equal to university education in its delivery and content. The platform instructors were mostly veterans and were well trained in their subjects, including basic applied physics, mathematics, and map reading, all necessary for navigation and understanding aerodynamics. Our education focused solely on subjects relevant to our future careers as pilots, such as physics, with no additional courses included, only courses pertaining to flight and officer training.

The rest of the pre-flight instruction was used to help the Army determine those who may or may not have the academic ability to complete the course. It was possible to be released from the program on academic results. Personally, I didn't see anyone washed out academically; it was just something they held over our heads as motivation to pay attention and work hard.

However, most of the "weeding out" of those who had the potential to fail was done through West Point-type harassment and hazing. West Point was the United States Army Academy. We never knew quite what was going to hit us next.

EATING A 'SQUARE MEAL'

One of the first major accomplishments during the pre-flight phase was to learn how to eat like a future officer. Keeping in mind that everything we did was overemphasized, our drama started the moment we lined up to go into the mess hall for a meal.

At least two TAC officers were intercepting us as we lined up. The first time this happened involved the usual gaggle, one of us behind the other, all yakking away, thankful to relax a little. That stopped quickly.

TAC officers intercepted our platoon, one near the entrance as we arrived and the other midway through the line of candidates. Things went something like this in the usual, very loud, concise language.

"Candidates, you are no longer in basic training. You are now a warrant officer candidate. When you arrive at the mess hall, you will stop and maintain an arm's length behind the person in front of you. You will then immediately assume the position of parade rest. When the person in front of you has moved on toward the front of the line, you will come to the position of attention, move forward as required, come to the position of attention, and then parade rest again. There will be no talking whatsoever!"

For crying out loud, we couldn't even go for a meal without someone screaming down our necks. This was only the beginning. The line progressed until it finally reached the cafeteria-style method of sliding your tray along the steel rails. You had already picked up your cutlery and watched as your plate was loaded with whatever you asked for, then it was handed to you at the end of the line and you placed the plate on your tray. Thank goodness the food was 'outstanding,' in the military vernacular.

At least four TAC officers on the mess hall floor were waiting for us hapless, very confused candidates. They intercepted us immediately as we left the queue and started walking off with our trays.

"Candidate! What are you doing? Where are you going?"

It was only when being stopped that I took in the scene in front of me. There may have been 100 tables, each with four seats, with many already occupied, and the candidates were eating strangely. Some tables had anywhere between one to three candidates with their trays on the table, standing in front of their chairs at attention. They were silent, eyes straight forward. Again, the TAC officer spoke:

"Go to that table where you see three candidates standing at the position of attention."

I immediately started marching to 'that table.' Upon arrival, the TAC officer, with the usual yelling in my ear hole, explained the procedure.

"Candidate, when you arrive at a table, you will stand behind a vacant chair. You will place your tray on the table, step to the left side of your chair, and withdraw the chair backward until there is space to sit down. You will then stand at the edge of the table in front of your chair, at the position of attention, until all four positions are full. Once the last candidate to arrive has assumed the position of attention in front of his chair, he will call, 'Ready . . . seats!' Upon hearing this command, you will all simultaneously sit down at the position of attention with your fellow candidates. He was speaking in a rapid, staccato voice. It sounded as if he only took one breath to get all those instructions out, much like our drill sergeants spoke in basic training.

Believe me, I was listening intently to this routine and watching it happen all around me at the same time.

"Candidate," again the TAC officer started, "once you are seated, you will eat a square meal. You will remain at the position of attention while seated, put your food on your fork, you will then lift that fork straight up from the plate to the height of your mouth, and then, in a straight line, from above the center of your plate, deliver that bite into your gob. You will then return your fork in a straight line back to the same position above the plate. You will then lower the fork in a straight line down to the contents of your plate for another bite!"

So now I was learning the Army's definition of a square meal. Every movement was at a ninety-degree angle.

Again, the TAC officer said, "You will eat your entire meal in this fashion. If you are addressed by a TAC officer while sitting at your table, you will place your food back on the plate and address that TAC officer in the usual fashion!"

They had laid down the law. I still shake my head at the hijinks that the TAC officers got up to while we were trying to eat a meal.

We were constantly being corrected and harassed by this roving troop. Without warning, you would hear, "That wasn't a straight line. Do it again!" Or, "Where is your napkin, Candidate? Do you always leave it on the table while you are eating, like some kind of savage?" Or, "Where in the hell did you learn to hold your cutlery like that? Somebody show this redneck how he's supposed to hold a knife and fork. You, yes, you, you're holding your cutlery properly. Show this idiot how it's done."

They continued to roam through the crowd of tables, correcting, shouting, and grooming us constantly to be 'officers and gentlemen.'

There was one TAC officer whom I nicknamed 'The Menace.' Somebody let this fellow out of his cage because he loved to bully anyone he could lock eyes on. He would walk past someone eating, suddenly bend down with his face in front of theirs, and shout at the top of his voice, "Say rubber baby buggy bumpers!"

His victim, usually with a mouthful of food, would quickly swallow and try to repeat the little ditty.

More often than not, they failed to repeat it properly.

He would start again, "I told you to say rubber baby buggy bumpers, Candidate. Are you too stupid for that?"

Usually the hapless candidate would think about what he had to say before he opened his mouth and succeeded in the repetition. The Menace would keep shouting at the candidate until he said the phrase correctly. This went on through most of the meal.

The mess hall was so large that, fortunately, they did not select me for such a stupid barrage of words. But I did gain a dislike for The Menace and kept an eye out for him, employing maximum avoidance measures to stay out of his line of sight. Eating the square meal lasted the entire four weeks of pre-flight. That was the toughest school of etiquette I have ever experienced.

Once pre-flight was over, we were allowed to eat as we pleased, but by then our table manners were taken as a given. We were not above reproach but also took pride in practicing our new lifestyle.

ARE YOU SMILING AT ME?

During the pre-flight period of our training, there was no such thing as a weekend pass. They held us captive in our concrete caves, where we remained totally at the mercy of the TAC officers.

Any time we were approached by a TAC officer while walking down the hallway, when that TAC officer reached a distance of six feet away, we were required to 'brace.' At that distance, we had to hit the wall with our backs and stand straight with our heads, shoulders, backside, and heels touching the wall. Once we had assumed this position, we would shout the greeting of the day, keeping our eyes straight forward.

"Sir, Candidate so-and-so, good morning (or good evening), sir!"

One Saturday morning, a TAC officer I had not seen previously was coming toward me in our platoon's hallway while I was returning to my room. As per protocol, I braced the wall at the correct time and distance and shouted the greeting of the day: "Sir, Candidate Guay, good morning, sir!"

Of course, this TAC officer could not pass up a chance for a small hazing. He immediately placed himself in front of me, with about six inches between our belt buckles.

"Candidate, what are you doing in the hallway? Where were you going?"

When he finished the second question, I almost started laughing!

I am six-two. This TAC officer was every bit of five-two, and I could feel his small drops of spittle hitting my Adam's apple. While I was peering at the opposite wall about four inches over the top of his helmet, it just struck me as funny. I tried to hold back my laughter while explaining to the 'sir' that I was heading back to my room.

The TAC could see my half smile and was mortified! He added fuel to the fire of my situation by having to take a step back to look me in the face. Thank God I had stifled my laughter, but I could not resist grinning from ear to ear. He looked me square in the eye.

Mind you, I did not return his gaze, and he shouted at the top of his voice, "Are you laughing at me?"

I was in the shit now.

"Sir, Candidate Guay, no, sir!"

"Candidate!" The TAC officer was becoming visibly angry. "What is it you find so funny?"

"Sir Candidate Guay, nothing, sir," I said, failing to minimize my smile.

With that answer, he started yelling . . . There's no memory of what he was yelling about or what he said, but he definitely unleashed a full broadside on me. I was just standing there with a stupid smile on my face and couldn't wipe it off. I was in very dangerous territory.

"Candidate, follow me!" and off he marched. I followed him down the hallway and the central stairway to the landing. As we reached the first stairway landing and was about to continue downstairs, he stopped me.

"Halt," he said. "Right face."

It was then I beheld something that had never registered in my tiny brain. On the side wall in front of me was an enormous seven-foot-high-by-four-foot-wide mirror. He stepped beside me, facing me from my right side.

Then, in a voice that could be heard down both ends of the very long hallways, he said, "Candidate Guay, attention!"

I was standing in front of the mirror, about two feet away. I snapped to attention.

As I did so, he continued in a very loud and clear voice, "Now smile! You will remain at the position of attention, smiling into this mirror until I return at my leisure and dismiss you."

With that, he turned on his heel and went down the remaining stairs, disappearing for what turned out to be a very long time.

It was never hard for me to smile, as I always seemed to think I might occasionally not take things as seriously as I should. I checked the time on my watch without anyone noticing by turning my wrist slowly and looking at it backward in the mirror after waiting ten minutes.

The hilarious thing was the reaction of the people using the central staircase. Some would stop, look, and laugh as though I were a statue. Some giggled as they passed me. Other, more serious-natured people would simply pretend not to see me and walk past. One hour, two hours, then two-and-a-half hours passed.

I recalled the rules they taught us in basic training regarding standing at attention for long periods of time. Bend your knees, make slight movements with your knees, then return to the position of attention. If this wasn't done during a parade formation, you might pass out because of poor blood circulation.

At what I estimated to be the beginning of the third hour, having exhausted my cheek muscles, my little TAC officer appeared beside me.

"Candidate, stop smiling."

With that, I dropped my smile and felt a few twitches in my cheek muscles that were thanking me.

"Candidate, if I *ever* see you smile again, I will pull your pink slip and see if I can't get you eliminated from this program. You are dismissed!"

He disappeared down the stairwell with that last comment hanging in the air. I learned a valuable lesson that day. In some situations, it's more important to control yourself than to laugh, even if something is funny. But I enjoyed the experience!

THE TWO FRUITCAKES

FRUITCAKE NUMBER ONE

Each morning, we had mail call. Our lives were changing rapidly, but this time allowed us to reconnect with reality. It was always wonderful to hear from home. However, one of the no-nos regarding mail was receiving food. As the recipient names were being called out, some envelopes decorated with red lipstick blots and a perfume scent, a small rectangular package emerged from the big white mailbag.

As our TAC officer read out the name on the outside of the package, he was smiling. We had never seen this before. He was usually crawling down our necks, screaming at the top of his lungs.

The hapless candidate came to retrieve the package, and the TAC said in a loud voice, "Candidate, what do you think is in this package?"

The candidate's reply was too low to be heard by the rest of us.

Again, the TAC shouted, "Candidate, speak up like you've got a pair! What do you think is in the package?"

"Sir, Candidate Jones, it's a fruitcake, sir!"

The TAC asked if it was appropriate to send food through the mail.

"Sir, Candidate Jones, no, sir!"

"Candidate Jones, who sent you this fruitcake?" The TAC was drilling in, his smile becoming a little broader.

"Sir, Candidate Jones, my mother, sir!"

"And tell me, Candidate, have you told your mother not to send you food through the mail?" was the TACs' reply.

"Sir, Candidate Jones, no, sir. It never occurred to me!"

Now, the TAC was practically gleeful.

"You need a reminder to inform your family and friends that we don't get food through the mail. Is that an accurate assumption, Candidate?"

The candidate knew better than to argue with authority, especially his TAC officer in the US Army. "Sir, Candidate Jones, yes, sir."

"Okay, Candidate, unwrap your fruitcake." As we watched, I'm sure we all assumed it was about to be broken into bits and pieces, and handed around the formation. However, it didn't take long to be proven wrong about that.

"Candidate, that is a beautiful fruitcake, is it not?"

"Sir, Candidate Jones, yes, sir. It is a beautiful fruitcake!" the unsuspecting candidate replied.

"Candidate, I'm glad you agree with me." Then, with a voice of absolute authority and emphasis came the command, "Candidate Jones, eat it!"

Holy shit, we couldn't believe it. This poor individual stood for a second, staring into the eyes of the TAC. "Now!" the TAC screamed.

With that, Candidate Jones started at the corner of the cake, munching like he hadn't eaten for a year. We all watched him, some of us in total disbelief. The TAC stood there off to the side so we could all watch him, facing the formation, eat, and eat . . . and eat. It was slowly disappearing down his gullet. We could see his eyes watering as he ingested more than half of the fruitcake.

When he was about to finish, the TAC spoke, and again, I was mentally shaking my head. He told the candidate to throw away the rest and warn his loved ones not to send food by mail.

As Candidate Jones turned and walked to the nearest garbage can, I'm sure he was about to puke. I suspect most of us standing in that formation over fifty years later still remember exactly what happened that morning. We all wrote to friends and family, begging them not to send food in any shape, form, or fashion through the mail.

FRUITCAKE NUMBER TWO

Allow me to explain a few points about barracks life as a warrant officer candidate (WOC). Each candidate had a small closet and two drawers for storage of his clothing, shaving gear, et cetera. (See photo at beginning of the story.) Above his closet was a storage area for his personal items. We called it the security locker. We could secure this space with a padlock. TAC officers couldn't look into or touch the candidate's security locker unless it was already open or unlocked. If it was open during any kind of inspection, you and your possessions were fair game.

We were pretty much left to our devices during the weekend, even during Hell Week. However, at the discretion of any TAC officer in the company, they could pay you a visit during the weekend. This meant we did not know when TAC officers would magically pop out of the floor. Bad luck if you did not see him walking down your hallway. If anyone was in the hall and had to 'brace,' he would shout the greeting of the day at the top of his voice to warn those in their rooms.

One particular TAC officer had a very nasty reputation as a bully. You guessed it, The Menace. He was about six-foot-six. His head was so big that when he put on his shiny black tortoiseshell helmet liner, it looked like he had to line it with oil and squeeze it down. This man was pure evil! He was built like a lumberjack.

Our platoon was located one flight up the stairs, with a right turn upon reaching the hallway. My room was the first one on the right, with another room exactly opposite. Any time a candidate heard the command, "Inspection post!" during the weekend, each person in that room had to drop everything they were doing and stand at the head of their bunks at the position of attention, while the room commander took his position on the left side of the door in the hallway and addressed the TAC officer as the room's representative. I was the room commander of our room.

During the weekends, we took this free time polishing boots, studying, and doing other leisure activities. TAC officers visiting another's platoon area were a very infrequent occurrence. However, these past weeks they were doing their best to keep us off guard.

Without warning, that lovely sunny Saturday morning, we heard the hallway fill with a powerful voice resembling that of a two-ton walrus. "Inspection post!" I did not recognize the voice; all I knew was that it was very loud. As room commander, I immediately dropped my half-shined boots and jumped into the hallway beside the door to our room.

As I was assuming the brace position, I looked down the hallway, and within six feet of me stood the one person none of us ever wanted to see in our platoon area. And he had a great big grin on his face! Remember, if your security locker is open at the time of inspection, the TAC officer may investigate your belongings.

TAC Officer Menace took the few necessary steps and then, with a left turn, faced the room commander opposite ours. The room commander gave the mandatory greeting to the TAC officer.

"Sir, Candidate Jones, room 202 is prepared for inspection, sir."

But The Menace paid him no attention and went straight into the room.

"Oh, what have we here? An open security locker," he said, answering his own question.

He stood in front of the locker and, because he was so tall, did not have to grab a chair like many of us did to see its contents.

"Oh, my goodness, what's this, a box of laundry detergent? Let's see."

With that, he grabbed the box of soap powder and spread a large amount of its content across the heavily waxed floor, which would now require a re-wax once he left.

"Oh gosh, I spilled some!" He was grinning like his first child had just taken their first step! He then scanned around the room to see what other mischief he could conjure.

While this was going on, I was looking straight into the eyes of the room commander opposite me. He was about five-foot-four and had a standard WOC haircut, white sidewalls and a half-inch flattop, but his eyes were bugging out, and he was shaking all over. While this giant was wandering around in his room, he started sweating and continued shaking.

We couldn't speak to each other, so I gave him an enquiring look and moved my hands as if to say, "What's wrong?" He just stood there, his eyes practically out of their sockets, shaking and sweating.

The predator in room 202 was still harassing the two guys in the room while my friend across the hallway was shaking even more violently and sweating profusely. As TAC Officer Menace came out of the room, he turned to face the room commander. Immediately, he locked eyes with Candidate Jones.

He said firmly and harshly, "What the hell is the matter with you, Candidate? Are you sick? Why are you shaking and sweating like an old woman?" He asked all of these questions in rapid-fire succession, not allowing any of them to be answered individually.

The TAC officer moved straight into Candidate Jones's body space, totally overwhelming him physically. I'm sure he was exceptionally good at this, with lots of practice.

Now he was looking down onto the top of the candidate's head, shouting at the top of his lungs, "What . . . the hell . . . is wrong . . . with you?" pausing between these words for emphasis.

With this, Candidate Jones began to cry. He still had not said a word.

By now, he was a complete mess. "Sir, Candidate Jones," he blubbered, "nothing, sir!"

"Candidate, I can see that there is something terribly wrong with you. I'm going to ask you one more time: What . . . the hell . . . is wrong with you?"

Candidate Jones lifted his right arm and took a two-inch square of fruitcake from his armpit in response to the question. TAC Officer Menace was utterly ecstatic.

"Well, what in the world do we have here? A piece of fruitcake! Are you aware of the regulation prohibiting food storage in your security locker, Candidate?"

No sooner had the question been spoken than Candidate Jones's knees were buckling.

"Somebody, get this man a chair!" yelled the TAC.

With that command, one of his roommates quickly brought out a room chair. Candidate Jones immediately sat down, crying, holding the fruitcake in his hand, and shaking like I had never seen a human shake before. He was having a total meltdown.

"Candidate, you are not well. You are out of this program. Come with me!"

With that, TAC Officer Menace helped Candidate Jones stand up, and the two of them disappeared down the stairwell.

We never saw Candidate Jones again. I believe his roommates packed his gear in his duffel bag, which was picked up later for shipment.

If you stop to think about it, TAC Officer Menace did exactly what he was supposed to do: find those of us who would crack under pressure. It was just a terrible thing to see firsthand.

5. *Photo supplied by Author. WOC Richard Guay with his training helicopter, the Raven OH-23D.*

7

THE FLIGHT LINE

Having finished our four weeks of pre-flight—passed through the academic filter, the harassment, establishment of routine, and being made to feel like a cricket in the corner of a chicken yard with a one-eyed rooster peering down, ready to strike—it was with great delight we took our first bus ride out to Dempsey Heliport. This was the main heliport for Fort Wolters, Texas. We were then introduced to our flight commander and subsequently assigned to our instructor pilots, who were now civilian Vietnam veteran helicopter pilots employed by Southern Airways. Southern Airways had the major contract for many facilities and services rendered at Fort Wolters. Their instructor pilots were extremely competent and stuck to a tight flight syllabus.

Each instructor pilot (IP) was assigned three students. This was called a 'stick.' Each morning, a different member of the three students would have the flight out of Dempsey to the stage field, where our initial training was done. Once the instructor departed with that student, the rest of us were bussed out to the stage field to save flight time for the student handover. The last member of the stick would fly back to the field with the instructor after his period of instruction. It was a great system and worked extremely efficiently.

I'll never forget my first flight in a helicopter. I was absolutely terrified! The instructor was friendly, but I think he had trouble believing his eyes. As you can see from the diagram supplied (see Image No. 41), a helicopter must tip the nose downward in order to enter forward flight. As the helicopter increased its speed and climbed to cruise altitude, I stiffened and straightened my legs, pushing my feet out in front of me—without hitting the pedals—and straightening my back. Honest to God, it looked like I was going to fall out through the big plastic bubble in front of me, kind of like being tipped out of a bucket. I was truly frightened.

This earned me a reasonably stiff lecture from the instructor about the difference between perception and reality. He promised me I would not tip forward out of the helicopter through the bubble, hurdle through space at maximum velocity, and crater into the ground. I took a few deep breaths and relaxed as we climbed out and the horizon dropped beneath us for beautiful countryside views.

This first flight was the only 'freebie' any of us had. The instructor continued his patter for the entire flight, but it was more of a demonstration ride as to what could be done and what was expected of me and my fellow students during the course.

We flew out to one of the many stage fields, which was about twelve acres, with four paved asphalt lanes approximately 1,600 feet in length. Until we soloed, these stage fields were the total extent of our geographic flying boundaries. The first and most difficult maneuver to learn in a helicopter is how to hover over the same spot on the ground while maintaining an assigned height, with the nose of the aircraft pointing in the same direction.

Later in my flying career, I heard the best description ever of what it was like to attempt to hover a helicopter for the first time. "It's like trying to stand on a soccer ball!"

A QR Code photo of Mustang, (Stagefield 4),
Fort Wolters, Texas, copyright expired.

On the first day, the IP started to teach us the art of hovering. "Okay, let's do it the easy way. I'm going to bring the aircraft to a hover and give you the pedals that control the tail rotor. I want you to keep the nose pointing at the control tower. Now, place your feet on the pedals. Remember to be gentle and smooth with your movements," said the IP.

I lightly placed my feet on the pedals and watched the IP put his feet on the floor of the aircraft in front of him. With that statement, thinking about all the advice I had just received, I tried to be as gentle as possible, and began small, deliberate, smooth movements with my feet. *My God, it's working!* Then, slowly, without warning, the nose started turning to my right. I immediately began adding left pedal to keep the nose pointing at the tower. I did this rather well, actually. We held our height of approximately three feet above the ground. Then, the aircraft turned to the right. Once again, I had to immediately adjust the pedals, adding left pedal. This time, I added too much pedal, and as we spun to the left, I gently added right pedal until the nose was again pointed at the tower. Each time I turned the nose either right or left, the initial response was smooth, but I was stressed and overcontrolling. This meant that I was constantly jigging left and right until I finally started anticipating the change in direction and making smaller corrections. Eventually, I could hold the nose within two or three feet of the intended target.

"Okay, that wasn't too bad. I've got it," the IP said.

"You've got it," I said. This was standard procedure when handing control of the aircraft from one pilot to the other.

He landed the chopper in an open area not far from the control tower.

"Now I'm going to give you the cyclic control. I'll increase the power using the motorcycle grip throttle, which is on the end of the collective, and at the same time, I will increase the pitch in the main rotor, which will begin to lift us higher from the ground while maintaining our heading straight ahead using the pedals."

The IP then started a gentle upward pressure on the collective, while a noticeably louder sound came from the engine because it was working harder. He began increasing pressure on the left pedal because we were creating more torque (see Image No. 37). The aircraft gently broke contact with Mother Earth. Once we were at a three-foot hover, I heard, "You have the cyclic stick, just the cyclic," from the IP.

I began moving the cyclic control, trying to hold the helicopter over a small imaginary spot directly below us. We began drifting left and right. Each movement I put into the cyclic was too fast and too far. This resulted in overcontrolling the cyclic control stick between my legs. Instead of gently nudging it in the direction I wished the aircraft to travel, I finished up traversing at a rapid rate, much further than I intended to travel. Remember, the helicopter will fly in whatever direction the cyclic is placed: left, right, forward, or backward.

"You're moving the cyclic too quickly. Hold it gently. Just think about where you want to go, and that's what will happen. Take a breath and try to relax again," he said.

The whole time he spoke, I drifted in almost every direction within an imaginary 200-square-foot box.

"I've got it," he said.

"You've got it," came my reply.

He came to a hover again and said, "Okay, think about what you're doing, make slight movements on the cyclic, and look at least fifty feet away and directly in front of the aircraft. Don't look at the ground too close to the aircraft. It'll help smooth out your movements. You've got it," he said.

"I've got it,' came my reply.

Once again, I started drifting across the ground as if I were trying to fly while the helicopter was drunk.

"Nice and easy, gentle, smaller movements in the cyclic."

I was totally focused on the IP's patter, and lo and behold, the square I was imagining actually did become smaller. I tried to relax my muscles and start breathing again, and sure as eggs, I reduced the size of my invisible twenty-square-foot box to a circle about eight feet in diameter.

The IP turned his head toward me and looked me in the eye, "You did really well with that one. Remember, gently, slowly. Just think about it, and it will happen.

"Okay, now I'm going to give you control of the collective pitch"—see Image No. 36—"Just keep your feet on the floor. Remember, as you increase the collective, you will have to twist the throttle to the left and increase power. Conversely, when you reduce the collective pitch, you will need to decrease the power in the engine and roll the throttle back to the right. You see the tachometer?" he said while tapping on the glass cover over the instrument, which showed the engine revolutions per minute (rpm). "Keep the long needle in the green zone that's marked there. I'm going to keep my hand just over the throttle, just in case. Just keep it at this height over the ground."

Now, the pressure was really on. I was focusing hard on what I had just been told and certainly didn't wish to overspeed the engine. That being said, I increased the engine rpm to the mid-range on the green arc painted on the glass cover of the tachometer and slowly began pulling up on the collective while slightly increasing the throttle setting. I was practically staring at the tachometer, and suddenly saw the engine rpm drop below the green line as I increased the pitch a little too quickly as we started climbing rapidly. You could actually hear the engine changing the pitch of its growl.

"I got it," said the IP. With that, he lowered the collective control, and we descended from our twenty-foot-high hover back to the original height of three feet above the ground.

"Okay," he said, "don't worry about changing any altitude, high or low. Just keep us at this height."

Once again, hardly remembering to breathe, I tried to hold the aircraft at the correct height. There must have been other forces working against me because it was literally impossible. I would drift up, and then, in order to correct my height again, I would push down on the collective and race toward the earth. Of course, the only logical thing to do was pull back up on the collective.

"I got it," said the IP while the helicopter was climbing up like a lovesick angel. He once again reduced the hover height to the standard three-foot hover, stabilizing it for me again.

"Take a breath, relax your arms and legs, take a few deep breaths. Remember, all we want to do is to stay at the height we are now, make smooth movements when you have to make them, but make them small. Let the aircraft do the work, not your left arm. Okay, Candidate, I'm going to give you all three controls. Let's see what you can do now to hold this aircraft still." With that, the instructor came to a three-foot hover approximately a hundred yards from any standing obstacle. "Okay, you've got it."

I couldn't believe it. I really had all the controls *at once!* "I've got it," I replied. With that, the rodeo began!

When you get full control, the laws of physics immediately do their very best to kill you and your instructor. Imagine the helicopter is at the bottom of a large pendulum, and that is exactly how the helicopter behaves. You see, there's this thing called the pendular effect while you are trying to hover. Imagine a steel cable attached to the mast (a vertical steel pipe that the main rotor blades are attached to) with this cable about fifty feet long, anchored to an imaginary point in space about 100 feet above the area where we are trying to hover.

Initially, you start with what you consider to be small, controlled movements in any direction necessary to keep you over one spot. After four or five of these movements, you usually wind up perhaps arcing upward to an altitude of about thirty feet, then while staring straight up at the sky, you suddenly come to a stop! Then, because you know you will crash when you slide backward, you push forward on the cyclic control stick and make a huge input of pedal, pivoting on the main rotor mast and turning your nose toward the ground, causing you to race downward into an imminent nose-first crash. So you pull back on the cyclic again, starting your upward arc to a height of about forty feet.

Now you are nose-high, looking at the clouds at a very low altitude, and if you don't do something soon, you'll slide backward and stab your tail rotor into the ground. So, you spin the aircraft around using the pedals, which then puts you staring straight down at the ground again and racing to your death in a bone-crunching crash! This makes you pull back on the cyclic again and race upward through the arc, perhaps putting in a little left cyclic so that you slide to the left, still captured by the pendulum, up and down, and then reach the apogee of your arc. Now you're turning sideways, pivoting with your pedals, and trying to spear into the ground again, maybe by jamming the rotor into the ground sideways!

The sad part about this exercise is that it never stops until your instructor takes over the controls and comes to a rock-steady hover three feet over the ground, telling you to take a breath. It is hard to describe how I felt physiologically.

I was panting like a greyhound that's just won its first race. I am sure I was extremely pale and sweating, but it was really cold outside. My heart was doing about 180 beats a minute while the adrenaline swam around my whole body, and my blood was pumping madly through my pounding brain at such a volume that I could hear my pulse loudly in my ears. I was wondering if I hadn't already had a stroke! I took a quick look at my instructor pilot to read his face. He gave me a small smile because he had seen this happen with every single student he'd ever had.

"I think you've had enough for today. I'll hover over by the classroom. You go over and get Hendrix for his ride."

With that, the machine magically drifted exactly where it was meant to go, flown as it should be flown. We landed on a small concrete helipad near the classroom, with the tail boom pointed away from the pathway. One thing you must always be aware of when flying a helicopter is the location of the tail rotor. It is invisible when the main rotor is turning at full rpm, and many people have died walking into it.

The scenario you just read was typical of the lessons we got before learning to hover. It gives you some idea of the skills and coordination required to fly one of these wonderful machines. Not everyone is cut out for the job, but thankfully, most of us made it through the flight training program without being washed out because we couldn't hover. Unfortunately, I had not learned to hover inside the allowed fourteen-flight-hour time requirement and had a change of instructor pilots. This resulted in my solo flight a few days later.

THE AUTOROTATION

There were many other skills we had to acquire prior to being able to solo. However, the one that really sticks in my mind is the autorotation. This maneuver saved my life on more than one occasion and was performed whenever the engine failed in flight. It was only natural that we learned to land the aircraft without an engine before we soloed, in the event of an engine failure at any stage before or after our solo flight.

Dear reader, if we were flying along on a scenic flight somewhere in the world in a helicopter and the engine quit, could you tell me right now what would happen? During my entire career, virtually without fail, each time I asked this very question, every passenger replied that the aircraft would crash. I am living testimony that this is not the case.

We are going to walk through the maneuver that is performed should a helicopter have an engine failure and learn to glide to a safe landing using a flight school scenario detailing the art of helicopter autorotation.

Imagine that we are on a rural airstrip. There is no other traffic at the moment, so we're going to do the following: we take off on the runway heading while maintaining 60 knots climb airspeed, then execute a left circuit by maintaining runway heading to an altitude of 500 feet, then turn left 90 degrees, while maintaining our climb at 500 feet per minute, onto the crosswind leg of a circuit pattern. As we reach 1,000 feet altitude, continuing our climb, we turn left 90 degrees again, putting us parallel to the landing strip. Continuing our climb, we see that we have 1,200 feet coming up on the altimeter. At 1,100 feet, we begin to slowly increase our airspeed to 80 knots and adjust our engine power, leveling off at 1,200 feet. Theoretically, we are now the correct distance from the runway, established on the downwind leg of the circuit, maintaining the circuit height of 1,200 feet as we parallel the active runway.

When we are past the end of the runway, and the approach end threshold is approximately 45 degrees off our left shoulder and behind us, we initiate a left-hand turn of 90 degrees, maintaining 1,200 feet, holding this heading on the base leg until we know that a final 90-degree left-hand turn will line us up exactly on the centerline of the runway heading, tracking inbound overhead the approach end of the runway.

We have in our mind's eye an approximate angle of descent for the autorotative landing and plan to touch down approximately midway down the length of the runway. As we overfly the inbound end of the runway above the center line and reach the point at which we should begin the maneuver, we reduce the collective to the full down position and retard the engine throttle to flight idle rpm. This then places the aircraft in a simulated engine-out state.

We now begin a fairly rapid rate of descent. Each helicopter type has an engine-out glide path particular to its own design. We maintain trim using the turn and bank indicator, ensuring the aircraft's nose is pointing into the wind and our ground track is down the middle of the runway. We watch the rotor rpm, maintaining it in the green arc on the tachometer, and control our angle of descent with airspeed; we'll use sixty knots as our autorotative airspeed. Now that we have commenced the descent, we have a better idea of our glide path and where we will land on the runway.

From this point, we can make small adjustments in the rate and angle of descent in order that we may land exactly where we want. In this model of helicopter, the glide ratio is four feet forward to one foot down in altitude at the airspeed we are maintaining. This is a wonderful glide ratio to get where we want to go. Actually, it may surprise you, but the higher we are, the better off we are at locating a safe landing spot with minimum obstacles for touchdown.

We continue our descent, checking our instruments: trim (keeping the nose of the aircraft into the wind and ground track down the center line), airspeed still sixty knots, with rotor rpm in the green arc, continuing the descent toward our intended touchdown point. At the height of approximately fifty feet, we begin to 'flare' the aircraft by gently raising the attitude of the nose of the aircraft. This decreases the airspeed and causes the aircraft to begin a moderate descent. While maintaining a rather nose-high attitude, we ensure the main rotor is still in the green arc. At about ten feet of height, we pull what is known as initial pitch in the main rotor, while beginning to level the skids of the helicopter with the runway.

This maneuver has caused us to slow the helicopter's forward motion—done properly, it can stop all forward motion—and then level the skids. At approximately five to three feet of skid height, we initiate 'the cushion' using the remaining rotor rpm, and pitch in the main rotor system, causing a ground cushion to lower the aircraft to a touchdown gently. And there you have it.

While I was a helicopter instructor pilot in the US Army, I estimate that I have performed this maneuver over 3,000 times in the Bell 47, exactly like the ones used in the TV series *M*A*S*H*, the UH-1 Huey, as well as the US Army's version of the Bell 206 Jet Ranger, with no damage to any aircraft, ever.

Now you know why helicopter pilots don't wear parachutes! It was always just above our heads in the form of the beautiful main rotor. After thirty-five years of flying helicopters, I can assure you the system works perfectly.

MY SOLO FLIGHT

On the day I soloed, I was very ill with a high fever and felt terrible. However, this became a blessing in disguise, as many of my problems were the result of overemphasizing my control movements. This brief illness virtually forced me to slow down my control movements and thought processes, resulting in a smooth flight with my new instructor. After spending almost an hour of flight time at the stagefield reviewing the basic maneuvers, the IP landed on a pad near the tower, unbuckled his seat belt, gave me a big smile, and said, "I think you're ready for your solo flight. Remember, don't change lanes once you've turned inbound." With that last bit of advice, he stepped out of the aircraft and walked up the steps to the small control tower.

I felt elated that I was about to solo, frightened at the thought of flying without an IP, and thankful I had 'made it,' and all these emotions spread over me at the same moment like a warm blanket. My time had finally come. I wasn't being kicked out of the program.

While making the appropriate radio calls, I successfully flew the three full traffic patterns, landed to a hover at the end of my assigned lane, and taxied to the change-over helipad near the study room, landing the aircraft softly onto the pad. My IP was waiting there. He jumped into his seat, strapped himself in, and with a big smile gave me a firm handshake and a 'well done.'

I stepped out of the chopper, took a deep breath, and contemplated what I had just done. It's hard to describe the feeling of accomplishment and relief I experienced. Needless to say, I was quite proud of myself, and the world was a wonderful place.

When the bus left Dempsey, we went straight to the Holiday Inn at Mineral Wells, Texas, where I was unceremoniously hauled off the bus and tossed into the swimming pool, fully dressed, because I had soloed. This tradition had been carried out since day one at the commencement of Army aviation flight training at Fort Wolters, Texas. I was dripping wet, and I was ecstatic!

MOVING ALONG

Dear reader, what I have written so far are just a few excerpts of the training that I endured, but truth be told, I mostly enjoyed it. I can only suspect that with my having grown up with a military mindset my entire life the amount of discipline dished out in training was easily received.

I'm sure there are many of you who have no wish to endure the degree of chastisement, control, and routine necessary to make one individual think and react in complete sync with the people around them in times of stress. It's not for everyone!

Let's see what happens when all of this training is put to use!

PART THREE

8

Wet season landscape, Republic of Vietnam.
Photo supplied by Patrick Mullen, Spartan 12, Stogie 13.

ARRIVING AT SAIGON, VIETNAM, SEPTEMBER 1969

The departure day for Vietnam came after finishing the mandated thirty-day leave. That morning, I had mixed emotions, full of excitement for what would come after nine months of flight school and saying goodbye to my entire family. There were lots of hugs, tears, and my mother's final words of advice delivered while holding my ears and pulling my face close to hers, "Don't you bring back one of them Vietnamese girls to this house!"

Of course, I said I wouldn't, which made her very happy, and she hugged me like there was no tomorrow. After saying the final goodbyes, I boarded the first leg of my journey at Gulfport, MS, Airport.

To tell the truth, I was exploding with excitement. Launching oneself into the totally unknown, much less into a warzone, truly is bewildering and, at the same time, electrifying. By now, tens of thousands of US soldiers had done what I was in the process of doing. Even though we all had the same destination during this life-changing odyssey, each of our thoughts was as different as our fingerprints. I never stopped to think that I had just 'signed the check' for my life in service to my country.

From Gulfport, I flew to New Orleans, Louisiana, then boarded a flight to San Francisco. After getting off the flight, having several hours to kill, I headed to the nearest exit gate. I spotted several other individuals in Army uniforms. I headed toward a small group of these soldiers, after which I bumped straight into a good friend from flight school. We had several hours to kill before boarding the helicopter to fly across San Francisco Bay to Travis Air Force Base for our ride to Vietnam. So, we jumped in a taxi and made our way into the heart of San Francisco to do a bit of sightseeing. At the appointed time, we returned to the airport. We boarded a sizable Sikorsky helicopter to fly across San Francisco Bay to our final stateside destination. Once there, after about an hour's wait, we boarded our Boeing 707 for Vietnam.

That airline flight was the quietest one I had ever experienced. I remember we reached Hawaii after dark for refueling. As we were departing, some of us managed to get some sleep.

When I woke, the sun was on the horizon, and we were three or four hours away from Saigon. If you could have read the minds of all of us on board, knowing that we were going to war, there would have been a sea of emotions sloshing around within that pressurized aluminum tube. I believe my being diagnosed with attention deficit hyperactivity disorder (ADHD) at the age of sixty-eight answered a lot of questions and, during this time in my life, was a tremendous psychological help. One of the symptoms of this disorder is not considering consequences, or in this case, not stressing out or worrying about what the future might hold. I was excited because I would finally put all that training to use and take the fight to the enemy.

Boy, did I have a lot to learn! I found myself staring out of the window of my Boeing 707 as it crossed from the ocean to the lush green landscape of South Vietnam. Suddenly, I was no longer tired from my trip. I could see a large river meandering through the middle of Saigon, Republic of South Vietnam, with its many tributaries escaping from its silver center into the surrounding network of streams and irrigation canals, visible almost to the horizon.

Surrounding Saigon was a beautiful montage of hundreds of lush, green, straight-lined rice paddies. The enormous city was encased in a thin dome of darkly polluted air.

As the airliner continued on its long final approach to a colossal Air Force runway, the array of military aircraft on both sides of the runway was incredible. Numerous assorted fighters, various cargo aircraft, and the ubiquitous UH-1 Huey helicopters lined up and down the flight line.

As per the usual drill, when our aircraft stopped on the tarmac and the 'fasten seat belt' light was extinguished, most of us jumped into the aisle as if it were a race to get out. As I recall, there was minimal hand-carry luggage. However, I do remember clutching my DD 201 file,(called the two oh one file). This was every soldier's personnel file, as it contained all personal information, including medical records, flight qualifications, any awards and decorations I had received, and things like that.

I remember a stewardess standing at the doorway, looking at us as we shuffled down the aisle toward the awaiting stairway to the war. She smiled and cried simultaneously, thanking us for flying the airline and wishing us well. You could see the sadness in her eyes. We then stepped onto the stairs to the concrete tarmac, clutching our files.

Because I hadn't been in a rush, there was already quite a long line leading to three men sitting side by side under a makeshift timber and tin roof structure under the shade of part of the airport's main roof overhang. I could see these men were reviewing our 201 files. We were all still reasonably quiet while standing in the glare and heat of the midday sun. Just about that time, a long line of what must have been Army infantry troops were boarding their flight out of Vietnam.

Their jungle fatigues were battered and faded; some wore cloth bush hats favored by the Australians, some just in a standard khaki uniform, but it wasn't just the clothes that made an impression on me. It was their expressionless faces. I wasn't familiar with the term '1,000-yard stare' then. But looking back, there it was, right in front of me.

These men looked terribly tired. Some were practically dragging their feet. I hoped it was simply a hangover from the celebrations the night before. Some were yelling at us over the noise of the aircraft turbine engines, as we were not far apart, but they were not smiling. This was the first time I heard someone call me a 'fucking new guy' (FNG). It was said with the intent to wound us, not share a joke. It was difficult not to stare.

There we stood for about another half hour until it finally came to my turn to hand over my file. My reviewer hardly looked up and said, "201 file," while holding his hand out like a beggar on a sidewalk. I handed him the file, and he flicked through it, looking for one piece of paper to determine my fate.

It was my qualifications page, and the information was on the top: my MOS (Military Occupation Specialty), 100 Bravo, or 100 B (Iroquois helicopter pilot). There you had it: I was a UH-1 Huey pilot. He started writing something on a small square of lined paper, then looked up as he handed it to me, telling me to report to building number so-and-so and remain there until my name appeared for a unit assignment on the bulletin board.

As he was an officer of higher rank than myself, I said, "Thank you, sir," as he waved his hand in a specific direction, which I immediately took note of, assuming that was in the direction of the building I should be looking for.

I then proceeded to the baggage pickup area to find my duffel bag. After asking a few questions and trusting my instincts, I finally found the building I thought I was about to inhabit for a few days before being assigned to a unit. The building was single-story, a typical Army barracks holding area.

On day four, the usual small group of arrivals was jockeying to read the notices on a large bulletin board near the entrance to the barracks. I was listening to the chatter of those in front of me, learning that the unit assignments had just been posted for the day. Several of us in front of the bulletin board knew each other. We each started reading different pages, looking for familiar names. Suddenly, I spotted my name, Warrant Officer 1 Richard R. Guay (WO1), and there it was, 190th Assault Helicopter Company, Bien Hao (Pronounced Ben Wah), III Corps. The questions I had in my mind about this company were almost identical to the other warrant officers around me. Where is it? What type of unit is it? Oh my God, what's it going to be like? At that moment, I was really excited. Suddenly, a loud voice came from behind, penetrating our collective gibberish.

"All of you assigned to Bien Hoa units, your bus is the first one in line over there on the right," the driver said while pointing at our bus.

Well, there you have it. We're only a bus ride away! We turned around and grabbed our duffel bags from the pile that had formed behind us, mounted them on our respective shoulders, and walked to the bus. It was painted OD green (olive drab green), the standard US Army color for everything.

We shoved our duffel bags into the cargo compartments comprising the bottom half of the bus and climbed aboard. At the time, we just realized that four helicopter units were stationed at Bien Hoa. The 68th Top Tigers, the gunships were called Mustangs; the 118th Thunderbirds, their gunships were call sign Bandits; the 190th Spartans, their gunships call sign Gladiators; and the 334th Playboys, which was an AH-1G Cobra gunship company. We were later to find out we were each a 'sister company' to the other, all in the same 145th Aviation Battalion.

I remember looking out the window and wondering aloud why the bus's windows were covered with such a heavy steel mesh. The bus pulled out on its journey to Bien Hoa as we all stared out of the windows, agog with wonder at the Southeast Asian city, the smells and the accompanying smog.

I had never seen so many motorcycles in one small place in my whole life. The streets were alive with them, with lots of pretty girls wearing conical white hats and the customary áo dài, a silk tunic with long pants. Those walking on the sidewalk looked very graceful and dignified. The bus continued to wind through the streets of Saigon, headed for Highway 1 and the forty-five-minute trip to Bien Hoa, a large town on the Dong Nai River.

Once we exited all the noise of the honking horns, the streams of motorcycles, and numerous pedestrians risking their lives on every corner, the countryside proved very quiet, beautiful, and a lovely silvery green. Hundreds of rice paddies were on both sides of the highway, as far as we could see, all full of blackish water with long, graceful reeds dancing back and forth in the gentle wind as we trundled toward our destination, north of Saigon.

The only people to be seen were children or adults riding on the backs of water buffalo alongside the road, tending the rice paddies. It was almost surreal looking out onto such a tranquil landscape and remembering all the terrible news footage we had watched on television for years regarding this beautiful country.

At last, the people alongside the road began increasing in numbers, the horn honking started again with numerous little blue and yellow Renault taxis leading the racket, and the motorcycle traffic increased to a ridiculous level. It was amazing to see a family of up to five with bags of possessions on a 125 cc Honda motorcycle! We continued through the streets on the way to our respective units.

I remember the first time I saw a Huey fly low-level over the top of us, headed down the same road we were on. We were trying to guess what was sticking out of the sides of the Huey and concluded they were rescue winches. Holy smoke, were we ever stupid! Of course, they were the M-60 machine guns, those excellent 'defensive' weapons.

The trip was totally without incident, for which, to this day, I am very thankful. The heavy steel mesh was over the bus windows because the Viet Cong (VC) had been lobbing grenades into buses full of American GIs while they drove through the streets of Saigon in slow traffic.

The beautiful open rice paddy areas were perfect ambush sites, and we were lucky. All in all, it was a rather idyllic introduction to a very war-torn country. I was soon to learn that Bien Hoa was only eighteen minutes north of Vietnam's capital by helicopter.

I was the epitome of a FNG and was told so several times during my first week. I was described as the most dangerous weapon the enemy had; completely unaware of our area of operations, couldn't pronounce town names, and needed help understanding the radio. I felt like I was 'lost in space.'

Like all assault helicopter companies, the primary troop transport helicopter (slick) was the UH-1 Iroquois, nicknamed Huey (D and H models). The gunship platoon used the older UH-1 B-model Huey. Our company radio call sign for the two platoons of slick helicopters was Spartan. However the first platoon (plt.) was called Golden Flight, the second plt. was Platinum Flight., and the platoon of attack gunships was the Gladiators.

After hanging around my new unit for a few days, I was finally kitted out for my role as a US Army helicopter pilot in a combat zone, with a Smith & Wesson .38-caliber six-shot revolver, a bulletproof vest (chicken plate) weighing about fifteen pounds (ensuring a full day of heavy sweating), and my SPH-5 flight helmet. The helmet had a blue tinted drop visor to protect your eyes from the glare of the sun, or a clear visor which allowed you to wear sunglasses and protect your eyes from flying shrapnel or bits of Plexiglas windshield in case it was hit by enemy ground fire. I chose the latter.

9

MY FIRST COMBAT ASSAULT

I was assigned as a co-pilot to a UH-1H slick going out the next morning on a combat assault (CA). When I saw my name on Operations assignment board, I felt a chill of anxiety, a charge of excitement, and a sense of joy. Finally, after a year of training, I was going to be given the chance to do what I came to Vietnam for: take the fight to the enemy.

The next morning, I was very excited and more than a little apprehensive. I devoured breakfast without throwing up from nerves, returned to my room, grabbed my gear, and virtually marched to the flight line.

There were crews scattered around the huge parking area, attending to their aircraft. I spent the next five minutes perusing the tail numbers of the choppers parked in long rows of revetments used to protect them from the explosions and shrapnel from rocket attacks. I located the tail number just as the sun had cracked the horizon. Little did I realize what was about to unfold.

I arrived at the correct UH-1 Huey slick, nicknamed a 'slick' because it only carried two M-60 machine guns on either side as a 'defensive' weapon. The crew was already there. I confirmed the time to make sure I was on time, but the crew didn't wait for me to do the pre-flight checks, because I was an FNG.

My aircraft commander (the AC), we'll call him Mr. Smith, was the same rank as me, but I was still required to address him as Mister. This signified his rank of warrant officer. He had already been 'in country' for nine months and was the 'firm but fair' type of individual. He sensed I was nervous but still allowed me to keep my dignity and didn't reel off all the Peter Pilot jokes he could have. Peter Pilot was another derogatory term for a FNG.

The crew chief and door gunner were also in the latter part of their twelve-month tours but reflected AC's attitude, probably more out of pity than respect. As we prepared for the start signal from our lead aircraft, I was told to sit in the right seat, shut up, listen, and not touch anything unless I was instructed to do so.

The noise level was staggering as fourteen Hueys started their engines and increased their main rotor speed to flight idle. The volume of radio chatter was amazing. We listened to three radios at once. Ultra-high frequency, or UHF, was for the aircraft-to-company operations office, located near the first hangar along a very long takeoff/departure lane. This radio had a long-range, covering many miles. Very high frequency (VHF) was aircraft-to-aircraft, being a 'line of sight' radio on our platoon frequency, and FM was usually reserved for communications with the infantry we worked with, used while in close proximity to the operator.

Finally, after each aircraft had checked their radios on the secure channel scrambler, our 'Gold Flight' (the First Platoon) began hovering backward out of their respective L-shaped five-feet-high steel revetments, lined up on their various departure lanes, and checked in with lead.

"Chalk 2 ready," "3 ready," "4," and so forth. "Gladiators ready." This procedure took less than thirty seconds on the VHF radio, then lead aircraft called the tower on the FM radio.

"Spartan tower, Spartan 483, flight of eight ready"—our platoon of six slicks with two Gladiator gunship escorts—"for departure."

"Spartan 483, Spartan tower, the winds are 120 degrees at 05 knots, altimeter setting two niner eight three, your flight of eight is cleared for takeoff." All of our departures were in one direction only, straight over the top of the city of Bien Hoa.

"Spartan 483, roger, flight come up staggered right," said Lead.

As the clearance was being given, the AC was increasing collective pitch; I felt the chopper getting light on its skids (fixed landing gear).

"Coming up," said the AC on the intercom.

"Clear up right," said the door gunner as he checked our clearance beside and behind the aircraft.

"Clear up left," said the crew chief, performing the same visual sweep.

The AC brought the aircraft to a hover, then hovered backward out of the revetment to line up with the departure lane's center line.

We 'pulled pitch' as soon as those from our flight in front of our position departed. We began hovering forward smoothly and entered our climb for the formation join-up at about 500 feet of altitude. All ACs had a chance to ensure their aircraft were flyable and returned to base for maintenance if needed. The weather was fantastic, and I was filled with a sense of anticipation and excitement.

The professionalism of this unit was outstanding. The Second Platoon, or Platinum Flight, departed immediately behind us, for operations with another infantry unit located to the west of Bien Hoa.

The sixteen helicopters departed Bien Hoa in two formations of six Hueys, each with an escort of two UH-1B Huey gunships. Our flight of eight flew south, past Saigon, to our area of operations, a fire support base near a village named Can Giuoc. The Second Platoon turned west toward the Parrot's Beak, near the Cambodian border, for their operations.

While en route, we flew at 2,000 feet of altitude, 500 feet above small arms range. We flew for thirty minutes and then landed on a dirt road to pick up US infantry troops. By now, it was about 0700 hrs. Our first load out was eight infantrymen with full packs and ammunition.

The slick platoon VHF radio was always busy with communication between the slicks and gunships. On our company frequency, the command-and-control ship (C & C) was already in orbit at approximately 3,000 feet above and near the intended landing zone (LZ) and on the company UHF radio. The FM radio was reserved for communications (comms) between the infantry unit we were about to drop off. Once the troops were on the ground, the two Gladiator attack helicopters would remain on site to protect the infantry.

A 'light-fire team' is the term used for the tactical fire support provided by the two gunships. The 'minigun ship,' which flew at a height of fifty feet above the ground or lower whenever engaging the enemy, had a door gunner and crew chief, each with 2,000 rounds of ammunition for their M-60 machine guns. The aircraft was equipped with two pylon-mounted six-barreled electrically operated Gatling guns (miniguns) on either side and held a total of 3,000 rounds of 7.62 mm ammunition per gun. A selector switch was used to choose 2,000 or 4,000 shots per minute rate of fire for the 'minis.' Mounted on the same pylons and inboard, the miniguns were two seven-shot rocket launchers (pods), each holding seven rockets with seventeen-pound warheads, each the equivalent of a 105 mm howitzer cannon impact.

The second gunship was configured as a 'hog.' It flew at an average altitude of 400 to 600 feet, following the minigun ship, protecting it from behind and above and providing supplementary rocket fire when needed. Its two nineteen-shot rocket pods were pylon-mounted on each side of the chopper. All rockets had the same seventeen-pound warhead. They also had their crew chief and door gunner seated behind the pilots in the cargo area, each with an M-60 machine gun suspended from a rubber bungee cord and 2,000 rounds of ammunition per gun. The machine guns fired 800 rounds per minute.

As we neared the landing zone, I could see gray puffs of 'suppressive' fire from US artillery rounds and hear the sudden *krump* of their explosions as they impacted the area we were about to occupy. C & C was on station above the intended landing area.

The terrain in this part of the delta region was all as flat as a billiard table, with canals dug by the French decades earlier crisscrossing the landscape. The glistening rice paddies with their elevated edges were literally everywhere. Everything was a beautiful green, but from our inbound altitude of 2,000 feet, we couldn't really tell which rice paddy we were to use for the troop drop. Also, bordering this area of rice paddies was a semi-cleared area of old jungle, probably cut down many years before.

When the flight was about a mile out, we had descended to 1,000 feet of altitude. The gunships dived from their escort positions on either side of our lift and roared toward the LZ. As they streaked toward the landing zone, we heard the C & C ship call a cease-fire to stop the suppressive artillery barrage.

"Redleg arty, Redleg arty, Spartan 6, cease-fire, cease-fire, cease-fire."

"Spartan 6, Redleg Arty, roger, cease-fire confirmed."

This rendered our LZ safe from 'friendly fire.'

As the gunships neared the intended landing point, with the minigun ship flying three feet above ground level at an airspeed of over 100 knots, the gunners started laying down a hail of suppressive fire. The Gladiator door gunner in the lead gunship was already holding a smoke grenade with the pin pulled in his right hand as he continued to fire. His tracers were visible in sweeping arcs, the bullets smacking into whatever suspected hiding places he could see that bordered the LZ.

After the C & C ship had vectored the lead gunship to the appropriate rice paddy, the radio call came from the C & C ship, "Gladiator, drop smoke."

"Roger," replied the Gladiator pilot as his door gunner released the yellow smoke grenade.

This created a huge plume of yellow smoke, thus giving the formation not only the landing area but wind speed and direction. The gunships then banked away and commenced climbing, one to the right, the other to the left side of the inbound formation.

When someone is firing on you, it looks as if a flash photo is being taken from a distance. The gunners were still firing to cover the gunships as they climbed, making sure they could engage any enemy muzzle flashes or tracer rounds, should they appear on the ground.

We continued toward the LZ, now losing altitude rapidly as we tightened our formation. I heard C & C instruct the flight to use full suppression. Lead repeated, "Flight, full suppression," "Chalk 2," "Chalk 3," "Chalk 4," "Chalk 5," "Chalk 6." Each aircraft commander acknowledged the command.

I heard the phrase 'full suppression,' which would be used far too often during my tour. It meant there was a strong possibility the VC were waiting for us. Then I watched and listened, but all I could hear was the constant *wop, wop, wop* of our rotor beat, and my heart booming in my ears!

I turned around and looked at the soldiers we were about to drop off. Stony faces, some sweating in fear, some just sitting there on their steel helmets, hoping for a little more protection in case we took any ground fire. I had never seen that expression before and never got used to it.

As we were inbound, passing through about 400 feet of altitude, the gunships had already begun rolling in on either side of the LZ, laying down a heavy barrage of minigun fire and rockets, shattering the ground around the border of the LZ. Hopefully, theoretically, the suppressive fire would keep the enemy's heads down while we were landing and departing.

The left side of the entire LZ was bordered by a thin stretch of jungle with the odd stump remaining from previous land clearing. They were scattered randomly and provided perfect places for the VC to hide while firing . . . and they were there.

At about fifty feet, the six Hueys flared, lifting the noses of their choppers to slow their airspeed for landing, while the flight leader yelled into the radio, "Commence firing!" With that command, all the gunners on either side of the aircraft started firing their M-60 machine guns at any suspected hiding positions, with long bursts of shattering explosions! The infantry had no warning of the full suppression, and they jumped or ducked, even though it was outgoing fire.

Now I knew what 'full suppression' meant. Suddenly, as we were about to touch down, my AC yelled into the intercom over the machine-gun fire, "Ride light!" I was shocked back into the current reality of the situation after watching all the surrounding chaos!

"What does that mean?" I yelled back at him.

"Get on the controls and ride light. If I get hit, you fly it out!" was the barely audible reply.

I immediately put my hands and feet on the flight controls with a featherlight touch. Just as our skids thumped onto the muddy surface, the crew chief and door gunner started screaming at the troops, "Get out, get out, get out!" The troops seemed to fly out of the big open doors on either side.

The amount of radio chatter was amazing. "Gladiators! Chalk 2 taking fire from the tree line, ten o'clock twenty meters!"

WUMP! A rocket exploded about five feet into the tree line exactly as directed. "Gladiators, Chalk 4 taking fire from a spider hole"—a trap door above a tunnel—"twenty meters, three o'clock!" *BBBRRRRRRRRRRRR*, the chainsaw sound of a tremendous burst of minigun came from the vicinity of the spider hole. The enemy fire was thick and fast from all around the formation. As troops cleared our aircraft, I saw a VC firing his AK-47 from behind a tree stump on the left. At that same moment, our crew chief spotted him and splintered the stump down to a nub with machine-gun fire as the VC seemed to disappear. Later, I was told he most probably dropped into a spider hole.

Just then, I heard the roar of miniguns firing at 4,000 rounds a minute outside my door on the right side of the flight and watched a long row of impacting bullets in a canal only twenty feet from my right shoulder. Each round threw water ten feet into the air! A rocket immediately followed this with a Doppler fuse, causing it to explode at a height of about twelve feet immediately outside my door.

It was so close to me that I could see the shrapnel pattern smack into the mud within a yard of me and felt a big *whack* on my face from the explosive concussion, followed by the acrid, potent smell of cordite as it seared my nose. Man, was I wired! This all happened in the space of about thirty seconds.

The lead ship announced, "Lead's out!"

As the last troops left his helicopter, you could hear his machine guns through the radio. We departed in a neat formation with our guns firing ahead of the infantry advance.

All this time, adrenaline was hammering through my body; I was still unconsciously 'riding light' on the controls! What a show! Several ships took many small arms hits, but no one was wounded or shot down. We continued outbound to return to the fire support base, pick up more troops, and do it all over again at the same location.

Mind you, the subsequent insertions were 'cold,' as the infantry we inserted had engaged the enemy and, with our gunships, mopped up what 'bad guys' they could kill or capture. The majority skittered away into their tunnel complex.

10

CALLING FOR EN-ROUTE ARTILLERY

'Calling for arty' is one of the very first things you do before you ever take off from anywhere, unless you're in the thick of an action. Artillery is large cannon fire. Sitting on the ground in the morning with the aircraft main rotor turning (turning and burning), you'd do all of your comms work with company frequency. Especially if you were flying a single ship on your own, you had to call Saigon artillery, or your nearest artillery information location selected from your daily issued signal operating instructions (SOI) used during your flight that day. This was done from a list of locations and frequencies used by artillery advisory stations.

After your initial contact, you would give them your flight route from your present location to your destination. They would plot your course on their map, then give you the name of any fire support base currently firing artillery crossing your flight path by the name of the fire support base, the azimuth of the firing (the direction the artillery was being fired on a 360-degree compass with 0 degrees being north, 90 degrees being east, et cetera), and a maximum altitude of the trajectory of the artillery round itself.

All of these fire support bases would be written on the plastic overlay on the tactical map you were holding in your lap as a copilot, with the dot representing the location and name of the fire support base. This was all written in grease pencil in case the fire base ceased to exist, or it was relocated.

1. A fire support base was the location of a battery of usually six artillery cannons. Their perimeter was surrounded by a large cleared area known as a killing zone, then interconnecting strings of barbed wire, which could also contain other anti-personnel explosive devices. Infantry units often either billeted inside the wire or were brought in the day before to rest in a secure area before being deployed in the near future for action elsewhere.

A typical call went like this: First, dial the FM frequency for Saigon artillery (arty), then initiate your call, "Saigon arty, Spartan 936 from Bien Hoa to Saigon." The reply would come almost immediately, and you better be ready to write quickly on the inside of the Huey windscreen with your grease pencil, or on the knee board you brought from the States.

"Spartan 936, Saigon arty. Fire Support Base Mary firing on azimuth 173, altitude 17,000; fire support base June firing azimuth 030, altitude 10,700; fire support base Black firing azimuth 273, altitude 15,300."

Sometimes, they would give you this information so quickly it sounded like they never took a breath. You learned to write your shorthand description very quickly. This information was essential, as aircraft had been shot down by huge artillery rounds crossing their flight path.

To continue, "Spartan 936, roger." This indicated that you were satisfied that you had copied and were responsible for the information. It was a given you would not cock this up because your aircraft commander would listen to every whisper coming from your lips in this environment. You would then put your finger on each of these fire support bases noted on your map and run the imaginary azimuth line in reference to your planned flight path and the altitude at which you would be flying, then determine if your flight path was safe regarding these rounds flying all over the damned place. Because most of our flying was done at 1,500 feet (minimum safe altitude for small arms fire), we were usually safe from the large volumes of artillery fire around us.

But we always looked for those fire support bases nearest our intended flight path and what direction they were firing regarding our track on the map. By the way, we never knew where these projectiles (rounds) were impacting, sort of a Russian roulette with the other end of the artillery trajectory (the impact point).

We occasionally found arty targets such as bunker complexes and were able to call artillery onto the targets, but not very often. The procedure was rather lengthy, so I chose not to cover that facet of fire. Suffice to say that the helicopters flying the skies of Vietnam were the eyes of a very effective web of lethal force.

Flight of four in trail formation.
Photo courtesy of Patrick J. Mullen, Spartan 12, Stogie 13.

11

FORMATION FLYING

To me, formation flying was absolutely thrilling. It was the only way we traveled from A to B as a platoon on combat assaults. Usually, each flight of four to six Hueys was different in its own way. The most common formations were staggered right and left, or trail. This allowed the safest distance between aircraft while remaining reasonably close together.

I mentioned before that the reason for formation flight was to encourage the enemy to 'flock shoot' instead of concentrating on one aircraft and watching his tracers as they were flying toward his targeted aircraft, allowing him to properly stitch one up and cause maximum damage.

As we departed the airfield, the type of formation was always dictated by the lead aircraft, usually piloted by our platoon commander and crew. As we left in the morning, say a flight of six Hueys, but up to twelve aircraft at times, lead would call on company VHF radio, "Lead's pulling"—pulling pitch for takeoff —"come up staggered right (or left)."

As lead, also known as Chalk 1, climbed out from the field, he would not only be taking up the heading toward our first pickup but doing so at the airspeed of only sixty knots. This was so the accompanying aircraft could catch up while cruising at eighty knots.

Then, the remainder of the flight would form up on lead, depending on the assigned formation. With aviation being a three-dimensional world, Chalk 2 would approach him slowly from the assigned side while maintaining the same altitude, and a forty-five-degree angle from his aircraft, by aligning the top part of his front cross tube with the rear cross tube of his landing skids. Chalk 2 would slowly approach, maintaining that line of sight until he was within one rotor disk, usually forty feet away from Chalk 1.

The following aircraft would perform the same maneuver from the appropriate side while approaching the second aircraft, or Chalk 2, and maintain the same approximate position relative to the distance between Chalk 1 and 2. This placed Chalk 3 directly behind Chalk 1, but over sixty feet of separation between the two.

O C1

O C2

O C3

O C4

Staggered Right Formation

We use several different formations from time to time other than staggered right or left. One was the echelon, either right or left from the lead ship. This was a succession of aircraft to the right or left, all on a forty-five-degree angle from the lead aircraft, still maintaining forty feet of distance between each aircraft. You often see this in formations filmed in many war films. The exception to the rule of separation was the length of one rotor blade, or twenty feet, if we needed to 'tighten up' for tactical reasons or had a small LZ.

O C1

O C2

O C3

Right Echelon Formation

Another formation we used frequently was trail (see photo on page 1 of this story). This was precisely what it sounded like, as the first aircraft approaching lead would remain exactly behind his aircraft, twenty feet from his tail rotor and the approaching aircraft's main rotor. I used to love trail formation because every time we hit any wind gust, I could see my main rotor chopping up and down behind the aircraft in front of me, knowing we were safe even though it looked like we weren't.

'One Rotor Blade Separation'

Photo courtesy of Patrick Mullen, Spartan 12, Stogie 13.

I lost a close friend from one of our sister companies at Bien Hoa. As the story goes, his flight was taking off from our battalion heliport. As they formed up, he thought he would get closer to the aircraft on his left while in a staggered right formation.

They began overlapping rotor blades as he approached, maintaining the forty-five-degree angle from his target aircraft. This is terribly dangerous because all it takes is a small puff of wind, an updraft or downdraft, and the main rotors from the different ships would make contact.

Sadly, that is precisely what happened on this beautiful blue-sky morning, with a bit of turbulence in the air. I was told by a witness that while the rotor blades were overlapping, the lower of the two ships hit an updraft, which bounced his aircraft straight up, causing both main rotors to collide.

Immediately upon their meeting, the shock of the impact of the two counter-rotating blades, each turning at 230 rpm, caused my friend's Huey to lose its main rotor, snapping the mast that held the main rotor blades. At the time of main rotor separation, his aircraft was at about 800 feet of altitude. It plummeted, nose first, to the earth. Everyone was killed instantly. The other aircraft lost approximately three feet from the tip of the damaged rotor blade.

The pilot at the controls of the other affected helicopter immediately lowered his collective as far as possible, starting a very steep descent. Because one of his rotors was now substantially heavier than the other, with one blade having lost its counterweight (which helped maintain rotor rpm in the event of an emergency) located in the tip of that main rotor, the cyclic control stick located between the pilot's legs, 'followed' the heavier blade, causing it to shake violently in a circular motion.

Incredibly, the pilot managed to hold on to the cyclic as it continued its frenzied, erratic, circular motion throughout the landing maneuver. He landed the aircraft safely with all crew members unharmed. He suffered a fractured wrist for his efforts, a small price to pay for saving himself and three others.

Another terrible loss of life that was simply due to pilot error.

More About Trail Formation

In my opinion, the most thrilling formation to fly was a trail. Keep in mind the pilot of the lead aircraft has the responsibility of not only where we are headed but also maintaining a smooth flight pattern, incorporating minimal control movements, knowing that everything he does regarding the movement of his aircraft will be multiplied proportionally by each following aircraft.

In trail, we used the length of one rotor blade as a measuring stick for clearance between aircraft. That's twenty-two feet, give or take. You can see from the photograph at the beginning of this story how close that really was. This is what made helicopter flying very exciting and, to me, worthwhile.

You can see the helicopters in front of you, all bobbing up and down in updrafts and downdrafts. However, there is still a safe enough distance between you to avoid being troubled, as long as everyone maintains the same airspeed.

As a pilot in this scenario, your primary concern was watching the aircraft's attitude (the relation of the aircraft's fuselage to the horizon) directly before you. For all intents and purposes, that pilot was also flying your chopper. The instant he changed his attitude, your attitude had to match his change. Imagine flying a tight trail formation, and you suddenly saw the nose lift on the aircraft you were following.

This meant two things: firstly, that aircraft would immediately start climbing, while at the same time losing airspeed. If you did not do exactly as it did, this would cause a midair collision with you chopping off his tail rotor and a portion of the tail boom, most certainly causing him to crash.

God only knows what would happen to your aircraft with all the bits and pieces flying into your windshield and other parts smashing into your chopper. You would most likely follow him in the plunge to your mutual deaths.

In another scenario, let's say that we are Chalk 4 in a flight of six aircraft. Trail formation was often used in very narrow landing zones. Say we are in trail, in a cruise configuration, all maintaining our eighty knots of airspeed, with another ten minutes to fly before we reach our intended landing point. While en route, we tend to spread out more, but never more than the forty-four feet dictated by our aircraft's total rotor disc diameter. It was always cool just watching how the helicopter in front of you kept bobbing up and down in the slightest bit of wind.

Then, when the radio traffic started between the command-and-control (C & C) ship and our flight's lead aircraft, we tightened the formation to within one rotor length, or half the usual distance used for cruise flight. It's fantastic how sharply your concentration tends to focus as you near the landing zone. By the time the C & C ship calls a cease-fire on the artillery prep that has been impacting your intended landing zone, the formation is locked in, rigidly tight. It seemed you 'could hardly pass a cigarette paper between aircraft!'

I also used to love it when we were going into an LZ with full suppression. As I mentioned, while flying inbound for an infantry insertion, once the full suppression command was given to lead by the C & C aircraft, the door gunners in the flight locked and loaded the 200-round small box of linked ammo, or 2,000-round belt of linked ammunition in their M-60s. Once the lead aircraft was at what he considered to be the correct distance from the intended landing point, he called, "Commence firing!" With that, the two M-60s in each aircraft opened up.

I assure you the volume of these two machine guns, each firing approximately 800 bullets a minute, is absolutely deafening. Any commands being given, or any communication going on inside your Huey, had to be forcefully shouted to be heard over the rapid explosions of these deadly weapons, even though we had the intercom system carrying our words between each of our helmets.

Whoever was piloting the aircraft at the time of the insertion was just absolutely wired! All you could think about was maintaining a safe distance from the helicopters around you, looking for the driest, flattest spot to land without smashing into another aircraft, and at the same time, scanning your immediate area for any muzzle flashes of weapons that might be firing in your general direction.

Once those skids hit the ground, the crew in the back would start screaming at the top of their lungs, "Get out! Get out! Get out!" This was a command for the infantry in case there was any question about when they were to exit the aircraft. Believe me, if there was any incoming fire, the US troops did not need much coaxing to go flat on the ground, and start returning fire once they were out of the door. Sometimes, if they weren't taking any fire, they would start walking or running toward the tree line. Still, you could see they always remained very vigilant.

The worst time for the troop carrying 'slick' Hueys was when the aircraft was approximately 200 feet from the ground at around 40 knots, slowing to a stop to allow your infantry troops to exit the chopper. The next worst time for a Huey crew was after the infantry had exited their aircraft. The flight would be lifting from zero airspeed until we were at about 500 feet of altitude and 80 knots of airspeed. The point is the lower altitude and slower airspeed presented our choppers as an almost unmissable target. Understandably, this was when most of our wounds, deaths, and shoot-downs occurred.

Depending on the day's requirements, a platoon of Hueys could be tasked to do this up to ten times, sometimes even more. Usually, the good part of this scenario was after the first and second insertions were done in the same area—the enemy had either been neutralized or had dropped down into their tunnels, living to fight another day. For our incredible slick drivers, the above scenarios were done day after day after day. It did not pay to think about the odds, one way or the other.

12

*Photo supplied by Collectors Firearms: www.collectorsfirearms.com,
.38-caliber Smith & Wesson Police Special.*

THE DAY JIM SHOT TIM

It was early December 1969, and our company had been given a maintenance stand-down day. This meant none of the pilots were flying that day, while their crew chiefs and hangar engineers were working on all of the choppers, clearing all the maintenance defects for the company fleet. Hence, all of us pilots enjoyed a day of rest and relaxation. Many wrote letters, some went to the officers club and drank too much all day—easy to do when the liquor was fifteen cents a shot. Others visited each other's rooms, talking and joking about whatever came to mind. As for myself, I loved to sleep in, get to breakfast at the last moment, go to the mess hall, order my favorite pancakes, two eggs over easy on top, with a stack of bacon, and smother everything with maple syrup. I'd then eat slowly, savoring every delicious bite.

After leaving the mess hall, I'd wander around looking for anyone to bullshit with, or go back to my room, write a letter, maybe take a nap, then go to lunch, and have a few drinks at the officers club bar, find someone to chat with, and wait for the 16mm movie of the night in the pool room.

My roommate, Tim H., and I arrived 'in country' within a week of each other in September 1969. He was an easy-going Virginian, a proper Southerner to his socks. He was about five-foot-eleven and a little chubby, with bright red hair. We shared a similar sense of humor and got on like a house on fire.

As the day was ending and dusk was at hand, Tim and I had decided to visit my best friend, Jim P., in his room. He was there, plus his roommate Gary, as well as a friend of Gary's I hadn't met. Things were a bit cramped in the six-by-eight-foot room. The accommodations were spartan in all our barracks' rooms: two steel-framed, wire-based single beds, one on either side of the room, with a small table and two chairs. The smaller rooms had one bunk bed, a table, and two chairs.

Jim's bed was behind the door, and he was sitting on the end closest to the entrance. Gary was sitting on the other bed with his friend from another flight company. I plopped myself on the other end of Jim's bed, and Tim pulled up a chair and leaned it back against the wall between the beds, facing the center of the room.

As pilots, each of us had been issued a .38-caliber Smith & Wesson Special revolver (commonly called a 38) as a 'sidearm,' which fired a slightly longer and more powerful bullet than the standard-sized .38 caliber. These pistols were seen in almost all the rooms, hanging in their holsters in various places, usually from a bedpost, locker handles, et cetera, for quick access.

It just so happened that Jim had his .38 out of its holster. He was popping the six-shot cylinder out, spinning it, and flicking it back into the pistol's body, thus locking it back into the firing position. The easiest way to describe this pistol model is that it looked like the six-shooter used in all the old Western movies.

I had grown up around guns of all kinds, being given a bolt-action .410 shotgun for my tenth birthday. My stepdad had a Hi Standard .22-caliber semi-automatic pistol, with which I became very accurate by the age of twelve, as well as a Browning twelve-gauge semi-automatic shotgun. I became such a good shot with the .22 pistol by age sixteen that I used it while hunting squirrels. For my sixteenth birthday, I was given a Marlin .22-caliber short-stroke lever-action rifle, and if I could see a target, I could hit it—end of story.

This intimate knowledge of weaponry and what they can do made me feel very uneasy that Jim was playing with a reasonably high-powered pistol in a room full of people.

"Jim," I said. "Sure as hell you're going to shoot somebody. Put that damned thing away."

He smiled at me and said, "When I grew up, no one in my family had a gun, especially me. I think it's cool, so I'm not putting it away."

Well, I figured he was nineteen years old, in a war zone, and doing what he damn well pleased. Who was I to tell him what to do? Then I saw him put a bullet in one of the chambers and snap the cylinder shut. Now I reckoned he was bordering on insane! I don't think anyone else knew he had loaded it.

"Jim, please put that thing away, for Christ's sake!" I implored.

He had the pistol in his lap and began pulling the trigger, counting the number of times the hammer fell on an empty chamber. He would reset the cylinder, counting the number of clicks he turned it backward. Then, pull the trigger X number of times, which would result in stopping one shy of firing the single bullet.

I saw what he was doing and begged him to put the pistol away. But he still refused, so I looked up and entered the conversation with the other guys. Then suddenly, *BOOM!* The pistol went off.

Then I heard Tim's head smack the wall behind him, and he said quietly, "Oh my God."

I had been looking down at the floor at the exact moment of impact and saw a spray of blood in the form of a long-dotted arch from the front of Tim's feet all the way to the door, approximately seven feet away. I didn't even look up. I just bolted from my spot and shot out of the room to find our platoon leader and organize our company medevac ship! The 93rd Evacuation Hospital in Long Binh was only a six-minute flight from Bien Hoa.

I was shaking like a leaf when I ran into the officers club, looking for our platoon commander to scramble the nighttime medevac helicopter. There was a live show on the stage at the time, so everything was at top volume. Spotting him at a table with some friends didn't take long. I hurried to his table and bent over so he could hear me over the live band.

I yelled in his ear, "Tim's been shot by Jim, and I think it must have hit him in the heart cause the blood went everywhere!"

His initial reaction was a smile and the word, "Bullshit!"

However, I put on my most sincere face and once again yelled over the loud band, "No! I think he may even have hit him in the heart!"

After briefly considering my words, he suddenly said, "Get the medevac ship cranked!" I asked him who was flying it, and scoured those holding up the bar to find the flyer.

We took the assignment as aircrew of the medevac ship seriously, so none of those assigned for the night had been drinking alcohol. Once I explained the situation, they took off like their asses were on fire!

Great, I thought, *now to get back to the scene of the accident and see how things are panning out.*

Upon entering Jim's room, I found two doctors squatting over Tim, one leaning over his head, the other behind him about even with his hips.

The doctor near his head was shouting rather loudly, "Where does it hurt?"

It seemed they couldn't find the entry wound.

Tim's only response was, "The pain, the pain."

Having worked as an ambulance attendant while waiting for my third term in university, my first thought when seeing Tim like this was that at least he was conscious and speaking, rather than remaining silent. It may sound strange, but I was more relieved than anything else.

He was stretched out on the floor, lying on his left side, angled sideways between the beds, and his feet were about four feet from the door into the room, where I was standing. He was bleeding profusely from a long gash across his forehead. At first, I thought it was a flesh wound, but I couldn't see a hole in the wall where the bullet should be if that were the case. I then realized the wound on his forehead was where he had struck the steel-framed bed. He probably thought he would fall into my lap as he fell forward, but because I had already flown from the room, he struck his head on the bed frame.

He had bled so much that a round pool of blood encircled his entire body from his head to the bottoms of his boots.

All he could say was, "Oh, the pain, the pain," repeatedly.

I stood there staring down at his face and saw the entry wound. It was midway in the center of his right lower jaw and, unlike the movies, difficult to see. It was a small purple line, the length of the bullet's width. I immediately showed the doctor nearest his head.

Then I looked around the room expecting to find Jim; however, he was not there.

"Where is Jim?" I called to no one in particular.

One of the rubberneckers standing just inside the door looked up at me and said, "I saw him running down the sidewalk toward the mess hall."

With that, I backed out of the doorway. I walked briskly toward the mess hall entrance, which was only about eighty feet away, around a corner made by the adjoining building. There, sitting on the concrete steps at the entrance to the mess hall, was my friend Jim. He was trembling worse than any human I had ever seen, attempting to light a cigarette.

The task proving impossible, I offered, "Here, give me the lighter."

He looked up at me, terrified, with eyes as big as dinner plates. He handed me the lighter and cigarette, still not speaking, shaking terribly. I lit the cigarette for him and placed it between his lips. He took a few calming drags before speaking.

"Is he dead?" he asked in a trembling voice.

"No, there are two doctors with him, and he's talking," I replied.

All my attention was focused on Jim. I had no idea what was happening back in the room.

At that very moment, Tim was being loaded onto a stretcher and taken to the flight line for his ride to the 93rd Evacuation Hospital. I suspect that his flight did not last more than four minutes, as the large helipad at the hospital was visible at a high hover from our airfield.

Jim was slowly calming down; his shaking was beginning to subside, but we still hadn't spoken much.

"I can't believe this happened. It was an accident," he said as his eyes darted left and right. I suspect he was waiting for someone to start looking for him.

Seeing he was starting to calm down a bit, I said, "I'll be back," as I wheeled and returned to the room at a trot.

Tim was no longer there, and as I approached the room, someone called out, "He's already been medevaced."

Thank God for that, was my first thought.

I joined the gaggle standing at the doorway to Jim's room, where the huge pool of blood remained as a testimony to the earlier events. It had not even been ten minutes since I had lit Jim's cigarette when the Criminal Investigation Division (CID) detectives showed up.

I don't believe any of us in that room at the time of the shooting were prepared for what was about to happen. I am trying to remember if there were three or four detectives; they were very senior in age, tough, and to the point.

Only one spoke, "Who fired the shot?"

"Warrant Officer 1 Jim P.," I replied.

All of us in the room at the time of the shooting were told not to speak with each other, ushered into separate rooms, and told to write statements detailing exactly everything that had happened.

The grilling from the CID was almost unbelievable and lasted three days. They did everything in their power to prove it was attempted murder. Each of us who participated in the investigation made it clear that it was nothing more than an accident. On the fourth day, they accepted our version of events and forwarded their conclusion that it was indeed an accident to the powers that be.

Because the incident was deemed to be an 'accident,' which means there was no need for a court-martial or similar proceeding, Jim was given Article 15 under the Uniform Code of Military Justice by our commanding officer.

This is an alternative to the court-martial process. Commanders can use this form of non-judicial punishment, avoiding a more severe form of punishment, to discipline service members, keeping the entire affair 'in-house.' Jim was punished with a twenty-dollar fine. However, such a punishment to an officer meant that he would never be promoted. Thus, it ended Jim's military career by preventing him from re-enlisting after his obligations to the government were met.

Over thirty years later, I found Jim via the internet and gave him a call. During the phone call, I mentioned our visit the day following the accident to see Tim at the hospital.

He asked, "Do you remember when he asked me to lean over to talk to me, and he whispered something in my ear?"

"Yes, I do," I replied.

"You know what he said to me?" he said in a humorous voice.

"Nope, I wouldn't have a clue," came my reply.

"I could barely hear him. He said, 'Thanks, man, I'm going home!'"

I could hear his smile over the phone, and I burst out laughing along with him.

Sadly, that one visit to the hospital was the last time I saw my roommate, with four tubes hanging from his throat to his abdomen, draining everywhere.

By the way, thank God it had been a .38- and not a .45-caliber pistol, or he may have lost his head. The bullet went through the right side of his jawbone, ricocheted off his upper left molars, tracked downward through his throat and esophagus, collapsed a lung, passed through his stomach, and then finally ceased its journey, lodging in his intestines. This resulted in the plethora of huge drain tubes that we saw the following day.

As a footnote, Jim continued to serve his country for the rest of his tour and, for his efforts, while spraying Agent Orange, flying just above the height of banana trees, was shot through the left hand, but chose to return to the unit when treated.

In the later stages of his life, he suffered greatly from post-traumatic stress disorder (PTSD) acquired from that ambush, as well as peripheral neuropathy. He died from several cumulative effects of Agent Orange, after being soaked in it while spraying the chemical using an agricultural boom device still used today for crop spraying.

I did see Tim's name listed in the Vietnam Helicopter Pilots Association membership book 2004, but unfortunately, I couldn't track him down. Someone said that he got a new set of teeth along with that 'million-dollar wound'—he was evacuated with a life-threatening wound, and not required to return to a combat zone, as it was then known. I have since learned that he passed away in 2007. Rest in peace, brother.

13

BAR STORY NUMBER ONE

AH-1G Cobra helicopter gunship.
Photo supplied by Patrick Mullen,
Spartan 12, Stogie 13.

OH-6A Cayuse observation
helicopter. Photo supplied by Patrick
Mullen, Spartan 12, Stogie 13.

This was the smallest turbine-engined helicopter in the US Army inventory until it was replaced by the OH-58 Kiowa, a larger, slower version of observation chopper.

The men crewing these tiny machines were among the bravest of the brave. Hovering 200 feet over jungle canopy, spreading branches with their rotor wash, looking for, and often finding, signs of enemy activity or the enemy troops themselves. Many were shot down and killed, or captured. In a way, those of us working with them, usually in the cavalry, considered them our heroes.

During the writing of my memoirs, many other memories come flooding back of stories that I heard, usually while having dinner with someone from another unit at the officers' club, or perhaps sitting at the bar enjoying a bourbon and Coke next to a very interesting person whom I'd never met before. The veracity of these stories might sometimes be questionable; however, they've always been most entertaining and, many times, extremely funny. The following story is one I will never forget, as it involved every emotion a helicopter pilot could experience in the space of five minutes.

One day, an Air Cavalry Red Team comprised of one low observation helicopter, or Loach, with a crew of one pilot and his door gunner sitting immediately behind him in the tiny passenger compartment, and two heavily armed Cobra gunships that were his overhead protection, were operating near the Cambodian border, directly west of Tay Ninh.

This area had several small roads leading from the Ho Chi Minh Trail (which continued south into IV Corps) and was the main highway for the North Vietnamese Army, transporting their supplies from North Vietnam all the way to the southern part of South Vietnam. It was for this reason that the air cavalry was scouting the area.

Apparently, the mission started with ordinary operations being followed. This meant that the Loach, or little bird, as they were also referred to, was flying slowly about three feet above the jungle canopy so that he might part the branches of the trees underneath his aircraft with the rotor wash and see what was below this thick, 200-foot-high, beautiful green carpet.

To help you keep things in context, it needs to be explained that these Loach aircraft flew with no doors installed on any exits. This was to aid passengers in escaping the aircraft should they crash. The helicopter was so small that the door gunner usually sat on a small seat, or the floor behind the pilot on the right-hand side of the aircraft, giving each of them the same field of view. The door gunner had his M-60 machine gun and usually a supply of 4,000 to 6,000 rounds, in 2,000-round cans. I flew as a Loach door gunner twice on my second tour. That will be covered in my next book!

It's worth mentioning that the degree of courage these young men displayed on a daily basis was almost beyond description, and they had earned the highest respect of almost any pilot in the US Army. While conducting their reconnaissance, moving slowly, usually hovering above the treetops, or just three feet off the ground, they often stopped for a good look. This presented one of the best targets of opportunity for the enemy armed with a deadly AK-47 machine gun, which was a standard issue for most Viet Cong and the North Vietnamese Army. The ammunition these weapons fired was high velocity and would go straight through a little bird or its occupants. It was very effective.

Keep in mind that while conversing with each other, the transmit switch for the radios was a trigger device under the pilot's index finger, on every helicopter cyclic control stick located between the pilot's legs. The radio traffic between the little bird and the two Cobras flying overhead gun cover, in a circular pattern at an altitude of approximately 1,500 feet, was often abbreviated, with numerical call signs used instead of wasting time with a company call sign. The little bird was in the first platoon of the Cavalry unit, and the Cobras were the third platoon in the Stogies. We'll say the flight leader was called Stogie 32, and the call sign of the little bird was Stogie 13. It would sound something like this:

"32, 13."

"Roger, 13, go ahead," replied 32.

"I got a hole in the canopy here. I'm going down to take a look."

"13, 32, that might not be a good idea!"

And this is how our story starts.

"13, we've gotta have eyes on you all the time! How the hell are we gonna know where you are?" said 32.

"Once I get down when I start moving out, I'll give you my heading and distance. That should work pretty well. I can get down fairly easily from here," said 13.

After about thirty seconds, the voice of the scout pilot came across the radio. "Christ! It's a four-lane highway! Okay, I'm in and going down!"

There was a period of silence while the Loach pilot continued to get even closer to the ground, maneuvering through the tree branches of the heavy canopy.

This brief silence would have been grinding the brains of the four Cobra pilots overhead, whose sole purpose in life was to keep this little bird crew alive.

"13, where are you?!" said the highly frustrated lead Cobra pilot.

When 13 replied, it was easy to tell he was panting slightly. "Holy shit, I got truck tracks, car tracks, and bicycle tracks still filling with water! They're going in both directions. I've gone twenty meters to the west. The canopy here is really high. I've got plenty of room to maneuver!"

In the Loach driver's mind, he could see the Cobras adjusting their orbits to the west. The jungle overhead was still very thick, and he knew he couldn't rely on his gunships should he get into trouble from below.

The tension in the cockpits of the Cobras was now measuring in the red. I suspect they were imagining the worst probable scenario. Losing a little bird under a thick jungle canopy was a nightmare in anyone's mind, but being responsible for the entire mission with such a thing happening would never be forgotten.

The next radio call from the scout pilot was utterly terrifying! The steady, high rate of fire could be heard blasting from the door gunner's M-60 without ceasing! *Ta ta ta ta ta ta ta ta ta ta,* then the voice of the little bird pilot could be heard while accidentally keying his microphone button. With the cadence of the M-60 still blasting away, his voice could be heard over the top of those rapid explosions, in a high soprano, screaming at the top of his lungs.

"Kill him, kill him, kill him!"

Ta ta ta ta ta ta ta ta ta ta ta ta! The cadence continued from the M-60 without letting up. The pilot's voice was now in an absolute frenzy, panting at such a rate it's a wonder he didn't hyperventilate and pass out!

Ta ta ta ta ta ta ta ta ta. "Kill him, kill him, kill him, kill him!" *Ta ta ta ta ta ta,* came the unrelenting, incredibly loud reports over the air ripping into their helmets.

The Cobra crew's hearts were palpitating while their breathing had become shallow and rapid, a demonstration of the extreme stress they were experiencing while wondering what the hell was going on. There was no point in keying their radio to ask the little bird pilot what was happening, as only a high-pitched squeal for both aircraft would result in their headsets. The scout pilot had not released the transmit trigger; he was still hanging on to the cyclic in what had to be his final death grip.

Suddenly, the firing stopped, but the panting continued wildly. One can only presume the scout pilot had not realized the radio was keyed for the whole encounter. He was still panting when he finally released the transmit button.

In an instant, the Cobra lead pilot yelled into the radio, "13, 13, are you okay? Are you okay?"

After a brief pause, the scout pilot keyed the mic again.

"Roger." For a moment, neither pilot spoke, and then it was the still-panting scout pilot again.

"It was a fuckin' monkey! It jumped up from a tree, grabbed my right ankle through the door, and snatched my foot off the right pedal. I couldn't get my left foot off the left pedal, and had it jammed full-on so he couldn't pull me out of the aircraft! We were spinning so fast that the centrifugal force was just too strong for my gunner to get the barrel up to shoot the bastard!! I don't know if he just let go, or we finally got 'm before we crashed! I'm gonna find a hole and get up there. We're going home."

The first time I heard this, I could not stop laughing! Imagine in your mind's eye a fairly large monkey with his arm in the door of a small helicopter, holding on to the pilot's ankle, slowly dragging him out of the machine while spinning so fast the monkey was level with the aircraft. The door gunner sitting one foot behind the pilot, fighting for the strength to pull the barrel of his weapon far enough forward to end the life of the creature that was surely going to send them both to hell! Tears just rolled down my face.

"Sons of Tyme," one of the best bands in Mississippi in 1968. From left to right: Don on bass, Richard (Author) on drums, Tom (our manager), James on lead guitar and vocals, Wayne Sharp on Hammond B-3 organ.

*Author at the age of ten years, Armed Forces Day, Eielson AFB, Alaska,
in the cockpit of USAF F-80C 'Shooting Star' jet fighter.*

*A3. Author with OH-23D Raven training
helicopter, the model he flew throughout
his training at Fort Wolters, Texas.*

*A4 My former roommate, 18
Year Old Warrant Officer 1 pilot,
Spartan 12 Stogie 13, Patrick
Mullen. Photo supplied by Patrick
Mullen, Spartan 12, Stogie 13.*

Low level in Delta Region with troops. Note smoke grenades on the post behind the soldier's head. Photo supplied by Patrick Mullen, Spartan 12, Stogie 13.

A four-ship, one-blade width left echelon formation. Photo supplied by Patrick Mullen, Spartan 12, Stogie 13.

Flight of 5 landing for refueling at Tan An. Photo Supplied by Patrick Mullen, Spartan 12, Stogie 13

7 ships shut down near artillery base standing by to pick up earlier inserted troops. Photo supplied by Patrick Mullen, Spartan 12, Stogie 13.

Unidentified recently extracted from combat action M-60 machine-gunner on left. He appears to have what we called the 1000-yard stare.Photo supplied by Patrick Mullen, Spartan 12, Stogie 13.

Ten ships on standby for troop pickup after morning insertions. Soldier helping with rice paddy irrigation.Photo supplied by Patrick Mullen, Spartan 12, Stogie 13.

Rear view of AH-1G Cobra gunship. Note very narrow body width of only 36 inches. A much smaller target to hit head-on. Photo supplied by Patrick Mullen, Spartan 12, Stogie 13.

The Colosseum in the foreground, the 190th AHC Parking Area.
Note the 'L' Shaped steel paneled parking revetments.
Photo supplied by Patrick Mullen, Spartan 12, Stogie 13.

CH-47 Chinook recovering a downed Huey for return to its' unit. This was
done whenever possible, as opposed to leaving downed aircraft scattered around
the countryside. Photo supplied by Patrick Mullen, Spartan 12, Stogie 13.

Air Force One with President Nixon and entourage visiting Vietnam. Our 190th Assault Helicopter Company always flew him and his party whenever in III Corps. Photo supplied by Patrick Mullen, Spartan 12, Stogie 13.

190th AHC VIP helicopter standing by for the Presidential Party. Photo supplied by Patrick Mullen, Spartan 12, Stogie 13.

190th Assault Helicopter
Company Spartan Patch

A16 190th Assault Helicopter Company
Gladiator, Gunship Platoon patch.

'Hooch Maid', each day our clothes and
uniforms were washed, boots polished, and
room tidied by our hooch maids. Photo supplied
by Patrick Mullen, Spartan 12, Stogie 13.

Patrick Fitzsimmons, Photo
courtesy of 190th Assault
Helicopter WebSite

Author Boresighting UH-1B Miniguns. Photo supplied by Author

14

VIET CONG 122 mm ROCKET LAUNCH TEAM

122 mm rocket. https://www.psywarrior.com/

O ne of the more common missions that the Gladiators had was to 'fly the wire.' What this meant was taking off at first light to fly the perimeter of Bien Hoa Air Base looking for any enemy activity, or hopefully catching a few of the stragglers from that night's infiltrators returning to the safety of their bases in the jungle. Sometimes, we would take off in pitch black with the minigun ship flying low at about 100 feet above the canopy, the hog ship flying behind and above us at 500 or 600 feet of altitude, providing covering fire should we take fire.

We had already had our breakfast, pre-flighted, refueled, and rearmed, and were hovering down the lane for takeoff from the Coliseum (the name we sometimes used to describe the 190th parking area) just as ten rockets began exploding uncomfortably close to the flight line.

"Gladiators, stand by for coordinates for the rocket launch site!" One of the more brilliant products of the Vietnam War was called anti-mortar radar. I don't know how it worked, but the results were almost instantaneous coordinates of any mortar or other launch site within range of its sweep.

Usually, these coordinates were passed to the nearest artillery base as quickly as possible, to destroy infrastructure in the immediate area, and any enemy within fifty meters of that launch site. Our light-fire team was given the coordinates this time, only about a six-minute flight away. Because the minigun ship was always the lead ship in the flight of two, I already had my grease pencil out, and when the coordinates came through, just as we were beginning to climb out, I wrote them on the inside of my windshield. I quickly plotted the location of the coordinates, and in the gray dawn light, we picked up the heading straight to the location.

This was a new experience for all of us, and just as we reached our cruise altitude of 100 feet, Ben, the aircraft commander, said, "Go guns hot, breakers in for the rockets."

I immediately looked up at the overhead circuit breaker panel and pushed in the minigun and rocket circuit breakers. This activated both systems. Ben pulled in as much power as possible without going into the red on the EGT (exhaust gas temperature) meter. We were in a hurry. The door gunners were locked and cocked as we approached a relatively sizable green field next to a small village. We commenced our descent from the edge of the jungle down to about three feet of altitude while the hog ship flew over for us.

As we slowed our airspeed, we began searching for anything indicating a rocket launch site. Just as we were pulling up to a slow hover, we couldn't believe our eyes!

Emerging from a small finger of some tall bamboo growing in a small creek immediately in front of us, a man dressed in a white shirt and black trousers and five women who looked like they were dressed for the office walked single file from the mouth of the small creek toward the village. To us, this was the rocket launch team, no doubt about it. Their faces were set not with fear but with determination. They marched straight at us, maintaining their single file. The ordinary civilian would have cowered in the face of such massive firepower being directed immediately at them at a range of fifty feet. Both door gunners were standing on the skids with the M-60s, ready to squeeze the triggers. These people did not veer and continued walking straight toward the village. Because there was no commissioned officer in either of our aircraft, I had to call company operations on the UHF radio for permission to kill.

"Ops, Gladiator 38."

"38, ops."

"Roger, we got five women and a man exiting a large ditch area near a village, and they're walking straight toward the village without stopping. We believe they're the rocket launch team. Request permission to kill."

While this radio chatter was going on, these people were marching one behind the other, doggedly and as quickly as they could without running, getting ever closer to the village. We were skimming the short grass in front of them, facing them in a big arc from left to right, trying to stop their progress, with no success.

Then came the most frustrating, but certainly not unusual, reply.

"Roger, stand by."

As gunship pilots, all our training and experience told us to 'fix' this situation right now. We knew we should have turned them over to the door gunners and killed them immediately.

We waited. As we waited, these six people were really moving, still one behind the other, as if in a parade, acting as if we weren't even there, headed for that village.

"Gladiator 38, ops," came the call we were standing by for.

"38, go ahead."

"Hold your fire, hold your fire!" came the twin commands.

None of us said anything to each other over the intercom, but we were damned angry.

"The local commander says they'll execute a combat assault on the village and do a search tomorrow."

"Gladiator 38, roger," was all Ben could say.

All of us were absolutely furious and disappointed. These people were the enemy in their deeds and conduct and should have been neutralized without hesitation. This was a really crazy war. We found out later that the combat assault on the village yielded nothing—what a surprise.

Ben selected the longest axis on the green field and executed our takeoff to return to flying the wire, with no results that day. We returned to the Coliseum, refueled, and shut down. Then, it was back to our ready shack to be scrambled if we were needed to support any infantry in our area of operations.

15

The Smell of Fear

.45-caliber ACP 1911 pistol. Image supplied by www.collectorsfirearms.com.

Our imaginations are as different as each of us. We don't even need to close our eyes to 'see' anything we wish to, be anywhere we wish to be, feel any emotion we wish to feel. We can escape, take part in, and experience anything we can imagine. Our emotions can be our best friend, neutral when observing a landscape in our mind, or they can generate absolutely mind-bending fear and anxiety.

In a theater of combat, our minds can give us confidence, courage, foresight, and anticipation, resulting in a feeling of satisfaction, or perceived satisfaction. Or the mind can kidnap our emotions and generate dread, terror, maybe panic, perhaps causing us to shake or tremble. It is just as easy to imagine something will have a terrible outcome as it is to imagine that you will be a total victor.

I'm sure that the professionals in the field of psychiatry could write a whole Ph.D. thesis on the above two paragraphs. What are we to think of someone who is about to enter what he or she suspects will be the last battle of their life, even imagining their own death?

In spite of all of the training that each of us received as soldiers and all the reassurances that this training is supposed to engender within our minds, which way will our psyche bend when we have been carried into the field of battle, with bullets ripping through the air past our heads?

Once again, each of us reacts in our own way. We have all seen movies where soldiers behave with either cowardice or bravery in response to a battlefield scenario.

After two tours of duty in the Vietnam war, and over three years of flying choppers for the government of the day in the Bougainville war in Papua New Guinea, my philosophy regarding being shot at is quite simple. If you are hit, deal with it. If you are missed, forget about it and get on with life. I never did join the 'What if?' club.

Any military organization will do everything in its power to train the highest number possible of troops to behave exactly alike. This generates reliability and anticipated conduct required under certain conditions, those troops working together for a common result, minimizing casualties, and maximizing positive outcomes on the battlefield.

All the training we received, beginning with basic training and following through each of our specialties for which we were trained as an end result, enabled a commanding officer to have a combined force that he can morph into a body that is amoeba-like, with a practically predetermined outcome. Imagine, if you will, the trench warfare from World War I. Line after line after line of trenches made by opposing sides, but those lines were predictable and effective at the time; the commanding officers of those troops could issue orders and achieve desired results as far as the movement of those soldiers was concerned, because the soldiers did as they were ordered. This is the result of the training they received before entering battle.

Where I am headed here can best be summed up in the following story.

As each of us arrived that morning for our daily aircraft inspection, we had already been told that we would be moving heaps of troops into War Zone D. Word was there were over 1,000 enemy troops there, with a fierce reputation. In a way, this was nothing new, but by the same token, it engendered the feeling of getting into a boxing ring with somebody bigger than you were.

We weren't discussing the pros and cons of where we were going. Instead, we just got on with the business of checking the general condition of our aircraft, feeling the amount of movement in different bearings in the linkages, checking the oil levels, opening and closing various panels all around the aircraft, and confirming everything was as good as it could be.

I was flying co-pilot in a slick aircraft (troop-carrying helicopter), which meant I was in the right front seat. We were a flight of ten aircraft, and as soon as the sun cleared the horizon, we cranked. After all the radio checks, we departed for our PZ (pickup zone). Flying in a formation of ten aircraft was slightly more demanding than our usual four to six aircraft for smaller lifts.

In a flight of ten aircraft, movement relative to the formation's size and shape was even more critical by the time we got to the last aircraft of the formation, known as 'Tail End Charlie.' In some ways, it was the most difficult position because the smallest movement of each aircraft in front of him had a cumulative result in a maximum correction of his aircraft attitude.

If the entire flight were smooth, well-coordinated, and tight, then Tail End Charlie looked just like the rest of the formation. If there were one or two aircraft even slightly exaggerating some of the control movements in a long line of ten aircraft, poor old Tail End Charlie was usually either dipping or raising his nose, sometimes dramatically, and looking rather ridiculous simply trying to maintain his position relative to the aircraft in front of him. Today was his lucky day. We were all pretty uptight and right on top of everything while maintaining our speed and distance from each other.

When we arrived at the PZ, the infantry was ready to board our aircraft. We had landed in a trail formation, each aircraft immediately behind the one in front. The infantry were in small groups in a straight, well-separated line we called a 'stick.' Our touchdown point was adjacent to the group corresponding to our position in the formation. After landing, Chalk 1 instructed us to shut down. No one ever asked why, but it was not uncommon. Hence, five minutes later, all the rotors had ceased turning. We were all sitting in our seats, not knowing when we would be told to start our engines, just chatting among ourselves, helmets off and quite casual.

The grunts (infantry) we were about to insert were sitting on the ground on our right side, doing the same as us, but rather subdued. Our load was about ten feet from the aircraft on our right side.

The one thing I noticed after a few minutes of chatting among ourselves was the smell. Initially, I couldn't put my finger on it, but I noticed that the infantry were not their usual selves. In fact, they were speaking very softly, if at all. I think they must have had the same intelligence briefing we did and were wondering what would happen to them.

The smell was fear. I've been told that animals can smell fear on you. I had no idea whether this was true up to this point. However, since that day, I have never doubted it. The slightly noticeable acrid smell was heavy in the air, very similar to armpit sweat, but from stress, not exercise.

Suddenly, with absolutely no warning, there was a very loud *BOOM!* It was just outside my door, and my neck snapped to the right so quickly that I almost left my eyeballs behind. It was a very close report of a weapon being fired. It's amazing what details you can see when you just had the shit frightened out of you. The shooter was about twenty years old, tall and skinny, with brown curly hair and a reasonably thick mustache; by then, he was sitting on his ass and sliding backward using his hands and left foot, dragging his right foot. He had shot himself through the right foot with his .45-caliber pistol. Make no mistake, this wound was self-inflicted. Now he would have to be medevaced to the nearest hospital, escaping a potential battle.

I had heard of this but never seen it. Personally, I didn't give it a second thought after all the immediate excitement of watching the performance. But it made me think, especially now, this much later in my life. Do I have the right to judge him? You bet your sweet ass I do. As Forrest Gump would say, "A coward is as a coward does." However, it just goes to show the power of the mind over the body. How terribly frightened this fellow must have been, letting his imagination run wild to the point of possibly facing a dishonorable discharge. How terribly sad.

16

HOVER HOLE TROOP MOVEMENTS

The demands made of troop transport pilots (slick drivers or slick pilots) were always varied and extremely formidable. The pressure on any FNG to learn the nuances required to not simply pilot his Huey, but to be able to control it with the touch of a feather, was immense and unceasing. Believe me, many variables were required to 'fly' the Huey with life-saving skill and technique. For example, put yourself in the right-side pilot seat, where the co-pilot sits in the US Army. Let's imagine a training scenario.

You're in a nice flat rice paddy full of tall rice plants, doing their very best to 'spill your lift' by dispersing your ground cushion, which is extremely important when you've got a heavy load of, say, ten fully kitted out troops, your fuel load on the high side, on a very hot day.

This hostile scenario would push your anus up around your neck, commonly known as the pucker factor. The above description was not uncommon, and believe me, you would be squeezing the top off the cyclic stick in your right hand, trying not to move your main rotor around too much, to avoid spreading your ground cushion all over the place, losing your all-important lift.

So, you are now on a paved flight line, looking down at a long white stripe that indicates the center of that flight line, with your chopper sitting on the ground. You have a full load of fuel, which will weigh well over a thousand pounds. You've packed in the necessary number of infantrymen with full pack, each averaging about 260 pounds. Depending on the model of the Huey that you were flying, you would be able to carry anywhere between three and ten troops. Believe me, every pilot in the company knew which of the aircraft were 'the pigs,' the weakest in the company. These aircraft could hold no more than three or four troops and still get the job done. Today's exercise in a UH-1D could hold about six or seven troops.

It's a typical hot day. The temperature is about 90 degrees Fahrenheit, and the humidity is about 90 percent. This is what is known as a high-density altitude day. In layman's terms, the air molecules are further apart than on a cold day, which means the rotor spinning above your head at 229 to 234 rpm is going to have to work a lot harder than on a cooler day.

As you begin to increase the pitch in the rotor blades with the collective, thus increasing your lift, the helicopter rises from the ground. You maintain the nose direction of the aircraft, looking straight down the white line with the tail rotor pedals. The main engine instruments you are watching are your exhaust gas temperature (EGT), or heat of the exhaust gasses; the N1, or percentage of available engine power being used; and the torque gauge, indicating the power available to perform whatever maneuver you are asking of the machine, as well as your main rotor revolutions per minute (rpm). This is a very abbreviated description of what's going on within the aircraft, and the myriad of instruments displayed within the helicopter instrument panel.

Photo by author, mockup of Huey Instrument Panel, U S Army Aviation Museum, Ft. Novocel, AL.

As the aircraft begins to rise from the ground, you find that you reach all your maximum limits on the instruments you are watching at a hover; your skids are only six inches above the ground. This is called the 'hover height.' This is enough for takeoff, but to simulate what really happens when every maneuver is critical, let's stress the aircraft a little more. You continue to increase the collective pitch, which increases the angle of attack in your main rotor blades. The helicopter will rise perhaps another twelve inches, but now you're overtorquing the rotor and drive system, your EGT is over the redline, as is the amount of torque you are pulling. Trying to hold the helicopter this distance from the ground with this load will usually result in overpitching. This means there is not enough power in the engine to continue turning the rotor at the required rpm. Eventually, within a few seconds, the main rotor will start to slow down, and your large, red low-rotor rpm light will come on with a very loud aural warning, a high-pitched whoop screaming in your ears.

Because you don't want to damage the machine in this circumstance, you will reduce the collective, thus reducing the pitch in the main rotor blades and the load on the entire drive system. This will result in returning to your six-inch hover, and all warnings will cease because the main rotor rpm will increase to the normal number of revolutions per minute, and needles on the gauges will go back into the green arc painted on the surface of the various instruments, indicating that you are safely operating the helicopter. Now, let's go to a real scenario.

EXTRACTING TROOPS THROUGH A HOVER HOLE

When we checked the aircraft assignment board that evening, it was not missed that we would be working in War Zone D, to the northeast of Xuan Loc in III Corps. We all knew that this was a very bad place to be. The first platoon of the Spartans 190th Assault Helicopter Company was designated as the Gold Flight; the second platoon was Platinum Flight. In true military fashion, each platoon had scarves in the appropriate color and wore them proudly. My scarf was gold. I would be flying co-pilot with one of the senior aircraft commanders, with whom I got on exceptionally well. I was very comfortable flying with his crew.

We knew our scheduled departure time and had performed all of our pre-flight checks, rearming, and refueling with the main rotor blade untied and ready to go. We were already in our seats, waiting for the signal from Chalk 1 to crank our engines. Both of us in the front seats had our eyes on Chalk 1's left door. It's hard to describe what my thoughts were.

We knew we were most likely flying into the throat of a hornet's nest, but just sitting there contemplating possible scenarios, none of which had happy endings, was, in my opinion, a waste of time. I just tried to clear my mind, almost like meditating, and relax. Whatever was about to unfold was going to happen, one way or the other, so why not maintain a calm demeanor, relax as much as possible, and have a clear mind should the shit hit the fan?

Right on time, Chalk 1's left hand appeared above his door, executing a rotating motion with his index finger pointing skyward. That's what the crews of eight Hueys were waiting for, the 'start your engines' or the 'crank' sign. With that, we switched on the battery and hit the start button on the end of the collective lever. I'll never forget the sound of that large turbine engine starting, which then started the main rotors beating the air into submission. The sound of eight Hueys with blades turning at full rpm was almost deafening if you were within fifty yards. However, as crewmen, all we heard was what was coming through the intercom system in our aircraft through the headsets in our helmets.

I might mention that all of our aircraft always flew with all doors removed. The large cargo doors for the aft passenger/cargo compartment were slid all the way back in a strong track and pinned alongside the fuselage. The two pilot doors in the front were completely removed. The exits were always open because, in the event of a crash, it would be easier to get out in a hurry. None of us had any false expectations that the doors provided any protection from gunfire. The aircraft skin was basically magnesium, which burned like hell, and you could easily push a screwdriver through it.

The good part was that we sat in ceramic-sandwiched, fully bulletproof seats, well cushioned and comfortable. The seats and the 'chicken plate' chest protector were made with a ceramic plate on the outside and a layer of metal internally. The aircraft commander sitting on the left side of the aircraft cockpit would slide the bulletproof panel forward, protecting his left side, from his waist to his neck, before hovering. The co-pilot in the right seat would slide his panel forward on his right, offering the same protection for both pilots. These bulletproof seats were composed of several separate panels.

The seat panel we sat on was reasonably large; the rear panel of the seat protected the backs of our bodies from the bottom of our backsides to just above the shoulders. On both sides, there were two smaller panels from the bottom of the seat panel up to about waist height. Two more panels were angled out from the back protective panel of the seats on each side, at an angle of about thirty degrees, as well as the two sliding panels previously mentioned, which allowed easy entry and exit from these bulletproof seats in and out of our respective left and right openings.

Courtesy of Patrick Mullen, Spartan 12, Stogie 13. Note
the rear and side panels of bulletproof seats.
Instruments show the aircraft is traveling at eighty knots of airspeed at approximately
800 feet altitude, with magnetic brake turned 'on,' for the flight controls! Note
the Configuration of the bullet-proof ceramic panels protecting the pilots.

We were told each panel could withstand the impact from three 7.62 mm bullets or one .50-caliber round, thus protecting us reasonably well. This did result in many pilots being shot in the legs, but our vital organs were theoretically protected from gunfire from beneath us. We were also provided a bulletproof chest plate weighing approximately fifteen pounds (the aforementioned 'chicken plate'), held in a heavy woven nylon pouch, which guaranteed heavy sweating all day. This was the only protection provided from small arms fire hitting us from the front. I always flew with my pistol in its holster between my legs. It made me feel a little bit safer. Although, in hindsight, I suspect that had it ever been hit by a rifle shot, it would have just created more shrapnel!

*Note the co-pilot in the right seat with his visor down
looking over his bulletproof panels.
Photo courtesy of Patrick Mullen, Spartan 12, and Stogie 13.*

We began our radio checks once all the aircraft in the flight of eight ships started. All First Platoon aircraft were on their discrete platoon VHF radio. A few minutes after the 'engine start' signal from the lead, his radio call came through.

"Gold flight, this is Lead, radio check."

"Chalk 2," "3," "4," "5," "6," "7," "8," came the calls in staccato succession.

We continued the routine while we were still sitting in our revetments by switching to our secure channel radio and conducting a similar communications check, but this time with operations. This tested the secret and discrete frequency channel through a totally separate radio, which scrambled the signal so that only the same type of radio receiving the signal would have the same coded information and deliver what, for all intents and purposes, was a standard radio transmission. This was just a little scratchier when you heard it.

"Spartan ops, Chalk 1 on secure, how do you copy?"

"Chalk 1, Spartan ops, loud and clear."

Once again, in their order, the flight of eight Hueys confirmed that their secure radio was operating correctly with a similar call.

Once this task was completed, another call from Lead came through,

"Golden Flight, this is Lead, Lead's pulling."

With that, Chalk 1 lifted to a three-foot hover and backed out of his steel revetment, with his crew clearing him to the rear and side while he was looking forward and clearing the hulking steel construction.

We were Chalk 3 that day, and when it was our turn in the order of departure, the AC said, "Coming up!"

"Clear up left and back," said the crew chief.

"Clear up right and back," said the door gunner.

With that, the AC lifted the aircraft to a three-foot hover and began backing out of the revetment until we were lined up on that long white line down the lane. As co-pilot, while we were backing from the revetment, my eyes were all over the instrument panel. I was checking all engine instruments, including the temperatures and pressures, the fuel load, and the tachometer.

As the tail boom began to swing to the left, we lined up on the departure heading, I called out, "Takeoff check complete."

With that, the aircraft commander said on the tower frequency,

"Spartan Tower, Spartan 627, Lane Two, ready for takeoff."

"Spartan 627, winds are 120 at 05 knots, altimeter 29.32, cleared for takeoff."

"Spartan 627, roger."

He then lowered the nose of the aircraft, and as we began hovering forward while increasing our speed, there was a slight dip as we entered translational lift, and we continued to accelerate our airspeed as we climbed out. (See Images 40 and 41)

Every day I flew in the Vietnam War, as the aircraft did its little dip while entering translational lift for the first takeoff of the day, I would think to myself, *You play the game, you take your chances.* This was my way of committing myself to whatever might come next. I never once worried about what 'might happen.' I was fully committed mentally and physically.

I think that having ADHD was, in many ways, a blessing for someone in my situation. As I mentioned before, one of the traits of this disorder is never considering consequences. Instead of worrying about 'what might happen,' I was thinking, *What's coming next?* I was ten feet tall, bulletproof, and my hair was on fire all day.

As was customary, the lead ship took up the route heading for our destination while maintaining an air speed of 60 knots and an altitude of 500 feet for the formation join-up.

"Flight, come up staggered right," said Lead.

From the time of departure to a final join-up would usually take between five to ten minutes while still traveling toward our destination. Once the last aircraft had joined the formation, he would call Lead on the VHF radio, "Tail End Charlie is in position."

"Lead, roger, rolling over to 080 knots."

We would then increase our airspeed to eighty knots smoothly and maintain the same neat and tidy formation while doing so. It should be mentioned that whoever flew the lead aircraft had to be exceptionally smooth when he changed any of the aircraft's attitudes (the relation of the aircraft's fuselage to the horizon), be it while increasing airspeed, any angle of bank, or any time he was descending or climbing, et cetera.

Flying formation and doing it properly was a real joy. Once the formation was formed, we increased our airspeed to 80 knots and climbed to an altitude of 2,000 feet, above the maximum small arms range. The entire time I was flying slicks, no one took any hits while we were en route. This only happened once we started the insertion or departure stage of the combat assault. Within a minute of takeoff, we had a beautiful formation on climb at eighty knots en route to the hover hole.

It was only a twenty-five-minute leg to the pickup point. The command-and-control helicopter was overhead at about 2,500 feet.

By now, we had all tuned to the infantry FM radio frequency and on UHF could hear the briefing going on between C & C and our lead aircraft.

Then, as we approached the area, Lead called on the infantry's FM radio frequency, "Pop smoke."

In about thirty seconds, we could see a bright yellow cloud rising through the dark green gap that was otherwise a uniform, emerald carpet of rainforest.

"Roger, I have banana," said Lead.

"Roger, yellow," came the reply from the infantry unit.

When we were about a mile from the hole, Lead transmitted on our VHF radio, "Gold flight orbit here. I'm breaking out for the approach."

With that, Lead commenced his descent and tracked toward the hole. The flight had maintained our altitude of 2,000 feet and started circling about a mile away, watching what was going on while listening to the FM radio. The smoke gave us the wind direction that we needed to know, which, in this case, was quite critical.

As Lead came to a hover at a height of about 200 feet in the center of the hole, he immediately commenced his descent.

"Flight, Lead, be advised that one tree on the eastern side of the hole is a bit close, but it's acceptable."

As we watched, his aircraft disappeared from sight. It was quiet on the radio now, as it should be. Radio silence was critical at these times if anything unforeseen happened. As we continued to circle, we could see our two company gunships, the Gladiators, in a tight racetrack pattern, making a small orbit in the vicinity of the hover hole in case anyone should take fire.

Lead's call came over the UHF radio, "Lead's loaded, coming out."

He was beginning his climb to hover up to the top of the 200-foot trees. Believe me; this is a high-pucker-factor maneuver. About forty seconds later, we could see the rotor blades of his aircraft as he rose to the top of the jungle, with the skids of his aircraft just clearing the treetops.

Once Lead had called that he was starting his climb, Chalk 2 had broken from the formation and was holding position about 100 yards from the hole with the wind on the nose of the aircraft and was ready as soon as Lead had cleared the treetops.

"Chalk 2 is in," was the radio call as he centered his aircraft in the hole and commenced his descent. Again, silence on the radios. We all waited, maintaining our orbit, keeping our eye on the aircraft's tail rotor in front of us, and maintaining our distance. Another call on UHF.

"Chalk 2 is coming up."

Again, with that call, it was our turn in Chalk 3 to break from the formation and take up our position while waiting for Chalk 2 to fly away. Because I was flying co-pilot that day, I expected the aircraft commander to do this maneuver. However, once we heard Chalk 2's call to come up, he said, "You've got it."

By now I had already been in slicks for about ten weeks, but I was still surprised that he would let me do the whole thing. I approached a holding point, waiting for Chalk 2 to reach the treetops and depart. As I started a small orbit while holding, I knew I had to 'stay ahead of the aircraft.' This meant my thoughts were mainly on staying steady on my controls, watching the altimeter as I descended, keeping an eye on the torque meter as well as a lookout for hostile branches. I knew I had to stay as calm as I possibly could and not tense up on the controls. Tension often led to rapid movement of the cyclic, with the resultant action of losing lift, and a possibly catastrophic result. So, I focused on my breathing, relaxed my shoulders as much as possible, and loosened my gorilla grip on the cyclic.

After Chalk 2's departure, I brought the aircraft into the center of the hole and came to a hover, just above treetop height. I could see how the infantry had cleared these LZ with det cord (detonation cord). Looking down, I could see as many as twenty tree stumps about three feet high, with a clear area in the center large enough to put the aircraft on the ground.

Det cord was an amazing invention. It was a white round wire, like a clothesline, about one-fourth inch in width, but was tremendously powerful when it exploded. I was told that a tree only needed one wrap of det cord for every inch of its diameter. Believe me, it was horribly effective. Now, getting back to the current situation.

While I was still up around 200 feet at the top of the trees, I picked a path for the tail boom while descending to keep clear of any obstacles.

As I commenced my descent, keeping the aircraft centered and well away from any of the tree branches that were flopping up and down trying to grab me, I looked forward, maintaining a level attitude, as well as glancing down left and right and keeping an eye on the height of the aircraft above the ground and any stray branches.

The crew chief and door gunner on either side of the aircraft continually informed me of the proximity of the closest trees during our descent. I could see that the infantry yet to be extracted had taken up position, which equated to either side of the aircraft once it was on the ground.

Continuing downward at a gradual pace, so as not to get into settling with power, I constantly checked the trees around me and listened to the crew for any instructions to help me maintain the proper clearances on the way down.

Being quite tense at this stage, I could feel the additional heat and humidity coming in through the door openings from the bottom of the jungle. I was sweating like a pig, with the salty droplets running into my eyes, but unable to do anything about it except blink and try to blow them away. As I approached the ground, I maintained a mental picture of where the tail boom should go.

I said over the intercom, "How are we going back there with the tail boom?"

"Clear down right, clear down left," came the reply from the crew chief and door gunner, who were hanging out and standing on the skids on their side. I gently lowered the aircraft into the three-foot-high grass and felt the ground start to take the weight of the aircraft.

With that, I began to relax and take a few deep breaths. I knew that everything I did was critical, and the last thing I needed was to destroy an aircraft at the bottom of a hover hole.

It was noisy with the infantry piling in, yelling at each other, vying for somewhere to sit, and then it suddenly got very quiet. I always enjoyed taking troops out of the war, even if temporarily. They looked terribly tired, and stunk to high heaven after goodness knew how long they had been in such a steamy, hot jungle. It was always good to turn around in my seat and get one or two smiles.

"Clear up left," came the call from the crew chief.

"Clear up right," came the call from the door gunner.

Glancing across at the aircraft commander (AC), I got a nod from a very straight face. I knew then I was cleared to perform a hover-up and departure.

"Coming up," I said over the intercom.

With that, I started increasing the pitch with the collective, and I felt the aircraft starting to get light on its skids. I checked that my controls were centered so I would be coming straight up, ensuring I did not drift in any direction. I could hear the engine beginning to roar while the rotor blades throbbed outside the aircraft, smashing the rotor wash into the grass and spilling a bit of my precious lift.

My eyes were glued to the torque meter while increasing the pitch in the rotor blades; the needle was heading toward the red background marker. I needed to break ground with at least five pounds of torque (available engine power) to get my heavy load to the top of the trees without using any ground cushion. If the indicator crossed into the red zone while doing my hover check, it meant that I would have to start leaving soldiers behind.

With great relief, as we started increasing our height, lifting to a hover, I could see that I still had perhaps four or five pounds of torque left. Once again, my eyes were everywhere at once, but mostly straight ahead and upward, planning my path, trying to stay as close as possible to use the same rising track that I used while descending.

Again, "Clear left," "Clear right," came the calls from the crew in the back as I continued to hover upward.

The whole time, the AC never said a word. I can assure you I was still quite tense. A very quick glance at the altimeter told me I was over halfway up, and I did not lift my eyes high enough to look for the top edge of the hole for fear of veering off in anything other than a directly vertical direction while maintaining clearance from all of the branches violently whipping in every direction around me.

Then, just as I began to clear the tallest treetops in front of me, that big red 'rotor low' rpm warning light came on with a very loud *whoop, whoop, whoop!* telling me that my main rotor was beginning to slow because I was pulling too much pitch.

"Just hold what you've got," said the AC. "Don't spill any lift."

I didn't move any of the controls. I was hardly breathing myself. Then, I could see the aircraft begin to lift, inches at a time, my skids gently rising, then down and back up out of the treetops. I must have caught a gentle puff of wind, lifting my aircraft maybe just one foot above the whipping treetops, and very, very gently, I pushed forward on the cyclic control.

My two best friends now were any lift that I might get from forward movement and a badly needed slight puff of wind on the nose; these would increase my clearance from the flailing branches beneath me. The skids were still touching the leaves of the thrashing branches in front of me, and the *whoop, whoop, whoop,* of the low rpm indicator was howling in my ears. Then, the aircraft began to move forward without losing any altitude.

Not so fast! Again, I started to sink, watching my rotor rpm, stopping my forward motion so as not to snag a skid on a branch, just hovering and praying. At least I wasn't sinking again, just holding my position, willing the 'low rotor' rpm horn to stop. I continued this small ballet dance as the aircraft began to sink slightly into the montage created by a solid green carpet trying to suck me down and destroy my aircraft.

Checking that my controls were centered again, I prayed for some form of lift. Sweat was pouring into my eyes. I had to consciously lighten my grip on the flight controls to avoid making any sudden movements. I must have picked up another small puff of wind just about that time. The aircraft rose, one foot, two feet, three feet. I began to gently ease forward on the cyclic, increasing my airspeed very slowly. I finally established a slow climb, which continued as I increased the airspeed and eventually went through translational lift.

That's when everything became good as a slight breeze entered the aircraft, starting to cool us down. I could feel my shoulders drooping and remembered to start breathing. Jesus Christ! I lowered the collective to decrease my now aerodynamically efficient rotor blades, silencing the aural warning.

The relief I felt was indescribable as the aircraft continued to climb out. I increased airspeed and took my precious load back to the drop-off point. I looked across at the AC. He saw my glance and said without any prompting, "You did a great job, Guay. I got it," as he took the controls and flew us back to the drop zone (DZ).

It was then that a great deal of relief washed over me. I stretched my legs, took several deep breaths, and wiped my brow with the back of my sleeve to stop the flow of sweat stinging my eyes. I have to confess I did feel great satisfaction and happiness at not having caused a disaster by sliding back down the hole to an unknown fate.

The last aircraft of the flight, Chalk 8, crashed. The pilot thought that he would try something different and, after loading up, apparently came to hover height just above the stump line, backed up to the edge of the widest part of the LZ, then dumped the nose while increasing to maximum power to try and actually go through translational lift and fly out of the LZ.

This was not a very good idea. From firsthand accounts, once he got to the other side of the LZ, he was going too fast to stop and hover but too slow to 'fly.' His only option was to pull the nose up, increasing his climb, 'flying' straight up the wall of trees underneath him while holding maximum power. That maneuver is called a cyclic climb, and this was not the time or place to try such a power-hungry maneuver. The inevitable happened. The laws of physics can never be broken without consequence. In the trade, we called it 'running out of pitch, power, and ideas' at the same time. The helicopter came to a dead stop while he was still less than halfway up, nose skyward.

He had to maintain his nose-up attitude while beginning to descend backward, and in a matter of a few seconds, had to use the tail boom for a pogo stick shock absorber. The tail boom collapsed and absorbed a great deal of the downward impact while the rotor blades smashed everything they could reach as the aircraft rolled over on its right side. No one was killed or badly injured.

That pilot wound up handing out boots and blankets in supply as soon as he got back to the company, and stayed there until he went home. I might mention he was not a warrant officer!

Happy to see the end of that day's flying, after dropping off our last load of troops, we returned to Bien Hoa. I had a long shower and knocked back several bourbon-and-Cokes that evening.

I have always been, and will always be, in awe of slick pilots and the incredibly difficult job they did on a daily basis. Not long after this flight, I did make UH-1 (Huey) Aircraft Commander, and at the end of my twelfth week in the country, I was transferred to the Gladiator gunship platoon, flying UH-1B Huey gunships. I returned to co-pilot status again until an aircraft commander slot was available in the Gladiator platoon.

17

AN ORDINARY,
SINGLE-SHIP DAY

The daily tasks for your average slick driver were many and varied. Just because you were part of an assault helicopter company didn't mean that every day would be a combat assault involving infantry insertions or extraction. Some days, you flew ash and trash, spending the day flying big yellow envelopes like an air mail delivery service. On Sundays, you could be flying White Robe Six, White Robe referring to God, and Six was the commanding officer in radio jargon. It was the expression we used for flying a priest around, usually to Special Forces bases so that he might deliver his sermons, perhaps five or six times a day. You might spend the day flying around some full colonel who had a series of meetings, exactly the same as corporate civilian VIP helicopters. We all got these jobs at least every other week. Some were almost boring, others quite demanding—it was the luck of the draw.

One particular day, my aircraft was assigned to extract a large number of South Vietnamese Army of the Republic of Vietnam (ARVN) bodies, the result of heavy infantry contact with the Viet Cong (VC). I wondered if the battle resulting in all of these bodies was still going on. If so, I would need gun cover. If not, no problem.

I was given the map coordinates of a small LZ where the dead had been placed in body bags, as well as the drop-off point for said bodies. As long as the PZ was 'cold'—that is, there was no firing going on—the assignment seemed to me like a walk in the park.

After getting the pre-flight done and fueling up, we were on our way, on a single-ship mission. It took us about thirty-five minutes to get to the initial coordinates of the pickup point. It was customary to always have your co-pilot with his tactical map in his lap and the tip of his index finger on your exact location.

The site was a small clearing with several large trees already having been felled to serve as a Huey landing site. Because we were dealing with the ARVN, I was not given a tactical FM radio frequency, but instead just proceeded to the small clearing, which already had body bags lined up, and landed so that they were just outside my cargo bay door.

Sure as eggs, there were plenty of them. A small crew was ready to load them into the back of the aircraft. I had taken on just enough fuel for three round trips just to make sure I wasn't overloaded with the first lift from an unknown LZ. I could see the takeoff path was nothing challenging.

After the first two or three bodies were thrown into the aircraft and stacked, I heard small arms fire coming from the same direction as the body bags. I paid particular attention to the sound, trying to gauge roughly how far away it was. It wasn't very close, and we weren't taking any hits, so I continued as instructed. Had the sound of the firing been any louder, I would not have landed without gunship cover.

After about eight bodies had been loaded into the back, I could see that the crew couldn't really stack them any higher, and I certainly didn't want to lose any out of our open cargo doors. I brought in the power and continued with my takeoff from the ground, straight out, breaking left away from the action, and climbed to 2,000 feet.

The drop-off point was approximately fifteen minutes away. Upon arrival, things went as planned, with the bodies being quickly removed from the back of the ship and laid out in a row near the landing site. I returned to the pickup point and continued with the second load.

Upon landing for the third pickup, after about five bodies had been laid across the floor, a wounded soldier, his chest and arm bandaged with his left arm strapped to the chest, jumped in and sat on the floor with his back pressed against the forward bulkhead behind the co-pilot, facing rearward. He had a smile as big as Texas on his face. I was absolutely infuriated at this development.

I started yelling at the door gunner, "Throw that little bastard out! Get rid of him!"

"Aw, come on, sir!" said the door gunner. "He's wounded. We can't just leave him here."

To tell you the truth, all I could think about at this point was my fuel load, and where I would have to go to drop him off at an ARVN evac pad, perhaps adding a refuel leg to the day's tasking. The original pile of bodies was still stacking up from the firefight in progress. It occurred to me I could leave him with the bodies and the ARVN. He was quite mobile and certainly didn't look critically wounded. Problem solved.

When the ARVN crew finished loading the aircraft, I immediately departed for the drop-off point. Upon landing, the young ARVN soldier jumped out while the roll call of the dead was being lined up, and he disappeared into the nearest large tent.

Upon returning for another pickup, only about six bags were left, and the senior ARVN on the loading party told me in sign language there were no further bodies. I was glad to see an end to the carnage and returned the last bodies to the drop-off point. Upon departure, I picked up my heading for Bien Hoa for a hot shower and a cold beer.

Dear reader, retelling this story reminded me of how little life could mean when you are totally immersed in an environment of constant exposure to death. How sad.

18

DIFFERENT TYPES OF
LANDING ZONES WET SEASON

*Wet season, Republic of South Vietnam. Photo supplied
by Patrick Mullen, Spartan 12, Stogie 13.*

Please bear in mind that where a flight would land a combat assault
was up to the 'powers that be' in the command-and-control (C
& C) chopper flying above the proposed action. The commanding
officers responsible for the results of these insertions were almost

always 2,000 to 3,000 feet above the action in their own dedicated Huey, supervising the entire action.

When landing in the jungle, insertions usually started with a very heavy artillery barrage of the selected area. When the inbound flight was approximately a mile away, they would call, "Cease-fire, cease-fire, cease-fire," to stop the artillery, allowing safe entry for the inbound formation.

During the wet season, when the rice crop of what looked like the geographical bottom half of Vietnam was well and truly growing madly in every direction, there were various-sized rice paddies. Man-made dikes bordered each other; they seemed to be touching for mile after mile.

The landing zones for various combat assaults would be indicated by a gunship flying low through the area and dropping a smoke grenade, indicating where the lead ship of the flight should land. During this wet season, and on such a flat landscape with no jungle and everything quite visible, the artillery bombardments prior to our landing were usually done away with. Our company gunships would always provide suppressive fire as we were making a final approach and would then stay on station and work with the infantry that had just been inserted if required.

I vividly remember that during the early part of my tour, we were doing a combat assault into huge rice paddy areas. The rice stalks and the depth of what looked like black, inky water were remarkably high.

On this particular day, the aircraft commander (AC) was letting me do most of the flying. Hence, I had eight US troops with full packs in the back cargo area of my H-model Huey.

The gunships had finished their suppressive fire, laying down heavy miniguns and rockets, while the door gunners fired along an imaginary line on either side of the landing formation. This was intended to keep the enemy's head down should they be there unseen. On this day, we were not taking any incoming fire.

On our first insertion, I flared the helicopter to a stop in a large rice paddy and was about to put the skids on the ground when everyone in the back started yelling! I couldn't understand a word because they were all yelling at once. I believe the aircraft commander was taking my measure in the situation and seeing what I would do, as he offered no solution and just sat there watching.

I lowered the chopper to put the skids on the muddy bottom, and all the screaming went up an octave. Finally, the aircraft commander shouted into the intercom, "They're telling you they don't want you to land here!"

The din in the back was absolutely incredible; the rest of the flight was just about to lift off, and I still had an aircraft full of troops. One of the infantrymen behind me leaned forward between the seats, looked me in the eye, and shouted,

"You're trying to land in a bomb crater, and it's probably twenty feet deep!"

Holy Christ, I thought, *that explains it.*

I remember hovering to my 10 o'clock. This is done by imagining 12 o'clock on your nose and the points of a clock from 1 to 12 in a circle surrounding you, from your right side around to your left, with 6 being directly behind you. I lowered the collective a little more to see if I could feel any earth beneath me, with the accompanying crescendo of screaming in the back, but there was no bottom to be found.

I then gently lifted the helicopter up until the skids were clear of the water and looked around for a direction I could safely maneuver without running into another aircraft. I wound up sliding well to my right and went down again, looking for the bottom. I might add that immediately the skids cleared the water, and we were hovering again. All of the shouting stopped completely.

They all realized that they had finally gotten the tactical situation through to me, and I was simply searching for the bottom in this very deep bomb crater. I went down into the water again about four feet, and still no bottom. I once again came up and, as there was still no aircraft on my right side, continued to hover farther away from the flight but still at the same Chalk position. I went down again. This time, I felt the bottom was only about three feet deep.

I said into the intercom, "Tell them to get out now!"

Immediately, my crew chief and door gunner started yelling, "Get out, get out, get out!"

I think the infantry were as happy to get out of the aircraft as I was happy to have them exiting.

Infantry being inserted in the Plane of Reeds. Photo Supplied by Patrick Mullen, Spartan 12, Stogie 13.

They splashed out of the helicopter and immediately started wading away from my aircraft toward other small groups of infantry, still slogging through all the deep mud and the high water. Thank God we weren't taking any fire.

Chalk 1 said into the VHF radio, "Lead's pulling."

I then focused all my attention on the loose gaggle of a formation that was now pulling up from the muck and flying away. As soon as all of us were clear of the water level, we started tightening up the formation in our usual fashion.

The one thing you always had to remember when you were jockeying to take your position in the formation was to never get below the aircraft in front of you.

Doing so would mean you were caught in his rotor wash while he was above you, pushing all that high-velocity air downward onto your aircraft rotor system, forcing you toward the ground. Once your ship became part of that downward airflow, it required a lot more of your available power to climb back above the extraordinarily strong turbulence.

The one good thing about the way the US Army did its training, even in a theater of war, was to let the co-pilot make mistakes and then be forced to work out a solution, with the aircraft commander acting as an observer only. Should the AC, out of necessity, be required to take the controls at any stage of the flight, well, it depended on his nature as to what happened next. When time allowed, most of them would spend a few minutes analyzing the problem with you and how you managed to get into such a predicament. But because they had to take controls, they didn't agree with your actions. Hence, your predicament would be explained in great detail. You were being given a one-time explanation of what was necessary to have avoided that situation. Keep in mind that as a co-pilot, I flew with a different AC almost every day, getting lots of varying advice, a treasure trove of knowledge at my fingertips.

The way you fly the aircraft, analyze your problems, initiate solutions, and fly correctly (or incorrectly) is called airmanship. It is a very broad term, but everyone knows what it means. Basically, it was a measure of the type of pilot you were.

If someone said you were having trouble with airmanship, it meant you were not doing very well at all. Airmanship was the one thing that each helicopter pilot had to exercise daily to the best of his ability. Every day you flew, you had to keep your mind open for something new. Every day flying in a war zone was like your first day of flight school.

Without a doubt, many of the aircraft commanders we had were some of the absolute best helicopter aviators in the world. More than a few were on their third successive twelve-month tour of duty and were skillful, knowledgeable, humble individuals. It was always an honor to be able to fly with them.

19

LANDING IN BURNING
RICE PADDIES

The takeoff time is 0630 hrs., and the wake-up time is probably 0500. The flight time for your first pickup is forty-five minutes to a fire support base where refueling is available. This is also the same location where you have to pick up the infantry that morning and bring them back later that afternoon. The weather is totally atrocious, and it's hot, with high humidity.

You've had your chicken plate on all day, which means your upper torso has been wrapped in a heavy nylon mesh while the outside air temperature averaged ninety degrees Fahrenheit. Staying hydrated was a challenge because there was no such thing as a CamelBak back then, and drinking hot Coke didn't seem to quench your thirst as it should.

After landing and shutting down for the pickup, the infantry comes pouring out of the gate of the fire support base for the first insertion. You're flying in a lift of ten Hueys. There are somewhere around eighty troops in this mob. You finally get your 'stick' of nine troops lined up just outside your aircraft, and they look hot, sweaty, pissed off, and perhaps frightened. They have no idea about what they're getting into. Only the coordinates of their destination, the call signs of the other infantry units they will be working with, plus the call signs of the gunships.

They're all goofing around while they pile into the aircraft. Those that are the quickest get to sit in the nylon webbing seat that runs the width of the rear of the cargo area; the rest line up and sit on the floor with their legs hanging out of the aircraft, three on each side. Each of the aircraft commanders are staring at the lead aircraft, waiting for the hand signal to crank up. Less than a minute later, a left arm appears from the door of the first aircraft, waving in a familiar circular pattern.

After each pilot calls out, "Clear!" he presses the start button at the end of his collective control, and the big turbine engines all start to whine simultaneously while the popping of the ignition plugs tick away, burning a constant fire in the bowels of their reliable engines. Slowly, the main rotor blades start to turn, as the engines continue to increase their rpm.

The early whine turns into a very loud scream as the rotors start their steady beat, automatically stopping their advance at idle speed; then, the pilots turn their twist grip throttles up to full rpm, causing the main rotors to reach their preset of 229 to 234 revolutions per minute.

Please join me now as I describe one of the more unusual occurrences in the life of a slick pilot.

"Flight, this is Lead, radio check."

Each aircraft then responded with his position in the formation. "2," "3," "4," "5," "6," "7," "8," "9," "10," came the sequenced reply.

"Roger, Lead's pulling."

All aircraft were already light on their skids, with quite a bit of pitch already being pulled, as they were near max gross load weight. The dust was not too bad, as they had landed on a small, well-packed dirt road leading to the fire support base.

The flight departure and join-up were routine as we continued our climb to 1,500 feet. The insertion point was only about a thirteen-minute flight. About a mile out, we could see a haze at the proposed drop-off point. As per usual, the gunships bolted ahead of the flight and commenced their suppressive fire. As we neared a touchdown zone, we could see that the gunship rockets had started several fires within our LZ, the smoke from burning rice stalks in the paddies was heavy. As we began to flare our aircraft for touchdown, we could see the flames still going in the rice paddies we were to land in. This did not happen every day. However, when it did, it was very unpleasant.

Just as we were coming to the bottom of our flare and about to level the aircraft for ground contact, the rotor wash had put out most of the small fires, but red-hot embers were flying everywhere, including down inside the back and front of our flight suits. Thank God we had visors to lower on our helmets, keeping these embers out of our eyes. But some still burned our faces with their tiny dots of incinerated vegetation.

We were squinting our eyes madly, but the visibility inside the smoke, the embers coming up in the air, and then the dust coming from the bottom of the dry rice paddy really kept us on our toes.

It's funny, but thinking back to this type of high-stress moment, I don't remember any type of specific emotion. The job at hand meant all I could or should do was to deal with each scenario as it occurred in a methodical, emotionless fashion. Hot embers in my flight suit, no big deal, not terminal. Very poor visibility, look at the toe of your skid. Where is the ground? No incoming bullets, no worries.

It seems that your mind goes into some sort of subconscious triage mode. Which task is most urgent? What is the second? What is the third? Solve it, solve it, solve it—deal with each incident as it happens, and go to the next one. Don't 'worry' or hesitate; just do! At that very moment, I was so busy dealing with trying to see through heavy smoke, small branding irons inside my shirt burning me, acrid smoke searing my lungs, and a huge squirt of adrenaline causing me to be hyper-alert. The last thing any of us needed was a hard landing, the consequences of which could range from flattened skids to bouncing into another aircraft with multiple fatalities. In short, I didn't have time to 'feel' any emotion because there was no room in my brain to risk any type of self-indulgence.

Just as soon as it was safe for the infantry to bail out, the crew in the back started their usual drill, screaming, "Get out, get out, get out!" Then the infantry joined the chaos on the ground, running as fast as they could, keeping their heads down so they didn't run into a tail rotor that would chop their heads off, then getting out of the fire as quickly as they could. It was total chaos.

Thank goodness we didn't take any ground fire. As soon as we were unloaded, we were waiting for those magic words, "Lead's pulling, come up staggered right." Immediately, we were all pulling pitch. Even though the smoke had thinned out because of all the rotor wash, now we were being belted around by updrafts from the hot air rapidly rising from the flaming surrounds. We were very careful to keep our lateral distance in order to avoid a midair collision. As we cleared the smoke, it was almost as if we had held our breath the whole time we were on the ground. We started breathing as though we had just come up from a 100-foot free dive.

We returned to the fire support base, picked up another load of troops, and returned to the previous location. As luck would have it, the next insertion was not in a burning rice paddy. Thank God for that!

20

The Angel at Can Tho

By now, I was an aircraft commander, having been 'in country' for about nine weeks. I relished the position and accompanying responsibilities. One day, our flight had spent the morning inserting US troops in a large geographic arc for a search-and-destroy mission southeast of Saigon. We had done a fair bit of work with several trips from the nearby fire support base to the insertion point, and we needed to refuel. We usually did this at the nearest large refueling point that could take up to six choppers at the same time.

In this case, our nearest base was a large airstrip that had been constructed with a major refueling point named Can Tho. It had a very wide gravel runway, and on the western side of the runway was what we called a fuel farm.

When we said, 'fuel farm,' we really meant that there was usually a large amount of fuel stored in rubber blivets, and the area was laid out with helipads already set up and the appropriate fuel hoses waiting for use at each of them.

Can Tho (if I remember correctly) had eight refueling points, so it was a logical choice from our last troop drop-off point, being the nearest purpose-built location. As we finished our last insertion, with no enemy action evident, Chalk 1 called for a staggered right formation, telling us we were heading for Can Tho. As we formed up and climbed to 2,000 feet, the usual bullshit started on the intercom.

Time always seemed to pass quicker if we were talking about our girlfriends back home or what so-and-so did the day before yesterday.

"Hey, Jones, you got a girlfriend?" I said into the intercom.

"Yes sir, we started going steady last year, just before I graduated from high school."

"She writing every week?" I asked.

"Yes, sir, up until about a month ago. I only got one letter this month," came the reply from the door gunner.

"Well, a dollar to a doughnut Jody's already knocked her up, and your 'Dear John' is already on the way," I replied.

This kind of needling would usually lighten the load psychologically for the whole crew. We needed to laugh as often as possible to cope with the stressful undertone of being in a constant 'anything can happen' mode every minute of every day.

As we were on a long final approach to the Can Tho airstrip, with no other aircraft at the location, Lead called our flight to a trail formation. This meant we could each land behind the other at our respective refueling points.

Our platoon commander was a serious-minded captain, a firm but fair career Army soldier. He liked things done in a very organized military fashion. Hence, we were still in trail formation when we came to a hover adjacent to our respective refuel pads, still facing the direction of flight.

On his command of "Right face," we did a right pedal turn simultaneously and hovered to our refueling pad, gently lowering our Hueys onto the concrete pads. We all took pride in this maneuver; we knew it looked good.

While in Vietnam, we all used the 'hot refueling' system. This meant the engines were not shut down and continued turning during the entire refuel cycle, with the pilots remaining at the controls and the aircraft was refueled by the crew chief or door gunner.

Once the refueller was back in the aircraft and had plugged his 'umbilical' cord into the intercom system, usually he would key his transmit button twice, each press sending a loud squelch sound through the intercom, informing the rest of the crew the refueling was complete, the fuel cap was correctly installed, and the aircraft was ready for flight.

As each aircraft finished refueling, we hovered across the runway to the opposite side, leaving the refueling pads clear for other choppers to use. This also allowed fixed-wing traffic a safe distance for landing and takeoff. We parked approximately one-half of the rotor disc diameter (about twenty feet) apart, in trail formation, shut down our engines, and tied down the main rotor blades.

Most days, we would remain parked in such a fashion until late in the afternoon when it was time to extract the troops and return them to their fire support base for the night, if they were that lucky.

The Can Tho airstrip was built on land as flat as that surrounding Fort Wolters, Texas, with no vegetation within miles. It was a boiling hot day, so some of us stayed in our aircraft with what little shade was provided, while others lined up under the shade of the tail boom or a fuselage.

The large rubber blivets were located on the opposite side of the runway. Each looked to be about twenty square feet and inside well-constructed dirt dykes, with interconnecting hoses. The blivets were approximately three feet high when they were full, so I estimate they each contained approximately 20,000 liters of JP-4 fuel (a fifty-fifty mixture of kerosene and gasoline). At least three of these large rubber monstrosities were side by side, paralleling the runway.

Not long after shutting down, a 20,000-liter fuel truck pulled up near the blivets, and the driver started transferring the fuel from the truck into the tanks, with his truck between us and the blivets.

We had been parked for approximately one-half hour when BOOM! There was a massive explosion. Immediately, I thought that it was a mortar round going off nearby and dove under my Huey! It must have taken me at least ten seconds to realize that I was sheltering from incoming mortar rounds underneath about 1,000 liters of JP-4 fuel contained in the fuel tanks of my aircraft. I scrambled out from underneath the aircraft and lay about thirty feet further away from the runway on my stomach, waiting for the next round to explode.

It was eerily quiet, no second explosion. After a few seconds, most of us stood up and looked in the direction of the explosion. The fuel truck was still there, across the runway and parked beside the blivets. Then, slowly, the refueller walked around from behind the rear of the truck, turning in a semicircle until he was facing our side of the runway.

He looked dazed and confused, with his arms extended straight out and parallel to the ground. He wasn't wearing a shirt, and all the flesh from both his arms seemed to melt and slough downward from his armpits to his wrists. The shape of this flesh resembled what one could imagine as a pair of angel wings paralleling the ground.

'The Angel of Can Tho.' Drawing by Katherine Nielsen.

He continued his slow walk toward us across the runway. I yelled at my door gunner,

"Bring him to our aircraft! We'll take him to the hospital pad!" and then turned and yelled in the direction of the lead aircraft, "I'm flying him to the nearest evac hospital." Then, turning to my co-pilot, I said, "Untie the blade. We're going!"

With that, I jumped into my seat, adjusted the throttle, and hit the start button just as the main rotor blade dipped down in front of me, indicating it was untied.

Listening to that reliable, beautiful sound of the turbine engine winding up, watching the blade start turning slowly at first, I then steadily rolled the throttle full on, bringing the rotor blades to full flight rpm. I yelled into the intercom, "Is everybody strapped in?"

"Roger!" called the crew chief.

Then, while my eyes scanned the instruments, I called into the intercom, "Are we clear of any incoming traffic?"

"Roger!" said my co-pilot.

I immediately departed at maximum power and headed to the nearest evacuation hospital, which I knew was about twelve minutes away.

After a few minutes, I turned around and looked at the patient. I immediately stared into his eyes. They were wide and absolutely blank, staring straight ahead, out through the Perspex windshield. I suspect his adrenaline was still blocking the excruciating pain he would be feeling shortly. I surmised he had done this task 100 times before but may have been smoking this time, and the fuel vapor had wafted into the ember in his mouth, causing it to ignite in a huge fireball.

Seeing this soldier in what could be a terminal condition was gut-wrenching. I tried not to think of the consequences he was facing. It looked like he might keep the skin on his face, but I suspect the heavier-than-air fuel vapors that exploded were, in fact, lower than his neck. He had already lost literally all the skin from his arms and his lower abdomen.

Bringing my attention back to the flight path I had chosen, I could see the large green tent with a huge red cross on a white background coming into view, and a big white H painted in the center of a concrete square nearby. I made a beeline toward it and came to a low hover, gently lowering the aircraft to the ground. By then, there were several people wheeling a trolley out.

One of them stood up on the toe of the landing skid outside my door so he could hear me over the roar and clatter of the engine and rotor. He stood there looking me in the face, and I yelled at the top of my lungs, "He was caught in a fuel vapor explosion!"

I'm pretty sure that description said it all. Because the soldier had his shirt off at the time of the explosion, I'm sure his back was in the same condition. I never looked.

I've only told this story a few times, but in my last twelve years in the profession of aviation, I was heavily involved in aircraft safety as well as refueling system audits. Thinking about that now, I realize why I must have had an overpowering urge to try and help others, so I would never have to experience what I saw in 1969 again.

21

22. WO1 Richard Guay 190th AHC Gladiators. Note 2,000
rounds of linked 7.62 mm ammunition in the ammo can beneath
his feet, for the door gunner. Photo supplied by Author.

FINALLY, I TRANSFERRED
TO THE GLADIATOR
GUNSHIP PLATOON!

I had no idea what the tasks of a helicopter pilot were when I arrived at Bien Hoa. The company policy at the 190th Assault Helicopter Company dictated that anyone wishing to join the gun platoon must first serve ninety days in slicks. Of course, if I had had my way, I would have been a 'gunny' the first day I brushed my teeth in the company shower block. My ADHD personality could not understand why I should wait three months to do what I felt I was destined to do the day I joined the Army.

In hindsight, those first ninety days were crucial for learning how to fly a helicopter properly in combat conditions. Still, that same period was used to evaluate any pilot wishing to join the gun platoon. Of course, I didn't realize any of the finer experience-based points in running an entire company with different platoons performing different tasks. Those ninety days were absolute gold in my career development.

The route laid out before me included the following points: understanding pronunciation of the Vietnamese locations, learning to think like a pilot whose circumstances could change in less than a second with the help of a bullet, developing airmanship that was beyond compare in the civilian world at such an early stage of experience, and coming to understand the way the infantry worked in a new helicopter warfare scenario.

I had to memorize frequencies that were used often in a day's aviation. I also had to learn the locations of many of the medevac pads for emergency medical evacuation, the nuances of leading a formation, and the ability to flight follow. Making calls for active artillery firing became second nature, and I learned in-flight emergency procedures like the back of my hand, developing a control touch that could determine whether I was going to crash or fly by simply moving the cyclic control unnecessarily and spilling a small amount of lift in critical situations (read 'Hover Down Troop Insertions' another memoir in this volume). I could quickly fill out a page in this book recounting how much I learned in those first ninety days.

At the risk of repeating myself, many of the points of evaluation of the individual potential gunship pilot included behavior under fire, knowledge of procedures required for movement with large numbers of aircraft nearby, not only the development or learning about critical control touch, but being forced to practice that knowledge practically every single day (every takeoff in a gunship was at max gross weight with fuel and ammunition), the development of proper radio procedures necessary to follow while taking fire (being shot at), and the method of articulating exactly the correct language and phrases used to maximize accurate return fire when under tremendous stress, learning everything about our weapons systems. In other words, procedures, procedures, procedures.

- For clarity, I'll explain the configuration of our company's two gunships.

The minigun ship was armed with two pylon-mounted electrically operated six-barrel Gatling guns known as 'miniguns.' They were mounted on the outboard portion of the pylons attached to the Huey. These guns operated on the Gatling principle of spinning the barrels, powered by small electric motors, and loading a bullet in each barrel as they spun at a preset speed (rounds per minute). Then, as the barrels advanced in their circular order, firing a shot in the top dead center of the revolution, extracting the brass cartridge, and turning until it was again loaded and fired.

The cycle continued for each of the six barrels. The speed of the barrels' spin determined the fire rate of these guns. The lower rate of fire was 2,000 bullets per minute (bpm) or 33 bullets per second, while the higher rate of fire was 4,000 bpm from each weapon; this was done with a selector switch. The ammunition supply was located in trays underneath the seat traversing the cargo bay. These ammunition (ammo) trays held 6,000 bullets of linked ammo, feeding the 3,000 bullets per gun through a metal chute.

Photo of gunship external armament. Courtesy of 190th AHC website. Each side of the aircraft has a seven-shot seventeen-pound warhead rocket pod and an M-134 7.62 mm minigun.

6,000 rounds of 7.62 mm minigun ammunition in UH-1B gunship.
Photo supplied by Author.

We configured our hog ships with two-by-nineteen-shot 2.75-inch Hydra folding fin aerial rockets (FFAR or rockets for short), each located on either side of the aircraft on external pylons. Of course, a door gunner and crew chief were aboard each hog with an M-60 machine gun for offense and defense purposes.

190th Assault Helicopter Company Gladiator 'Hog' ship.
Courtesy of 190th Assault Helicopter website.

We had our regular 0500 wake-up, a breakfast trip to the mess hall, and made our way to the flight line. The AC introduced me to the other crew when I arrived at my assigned minigun ship. Then, we did a walk-around inspection, as he explained the attaching points and method of operation of the miniguns and the rocket pods. He also showed me the operation of the minigun sight and explained the field of travel of the flexible minigun system.

The minigun sight was stowed above the co-pilot's head and attached to the upper edge of the windshield's steel frame. When released from its mount, it dropped down on a series of rods and stabilized immediately in front of my face. It had a pistol grip at the bottom, which fit nicely into my hand. The sighting device itself was a two-inch square of glass with a light dot inside a circle superimposed in the center. This configuration was called a

Flex minigun sight for UH-1 Huey gunship.
From www.174ahc.org website.
Photo by Jim McDaniel, 1967.

'pipper.' At the bottom of the handle was a small button that fit nicely under my little finger. When it was depressed, the hydraulically controlled miniguns would immediately flex exactly where the gunner was looking.

The author with the minigun sight extended, resetting the rocket firing circuit breaker during an actual engagement. Photo supplied by Author.

The trigger that fired the guns was a small black button under my index finger. Once I had the pipper on my target, I had to press the trigger button, and 4,000 bullets per minute would stream into the target. The linked ammo that we used had one tracer bullet (containing a red phosphorus charge), which ignited upon firing and would be visible for 700 meters, or virtually until the time of impact, followed by four ball bullets, which were invisible once fired.

Hence, when the miniguns were employed, it looked like a stream of red lead. We used the term 'hosing' a target, as that's precisely what it looks like when watering the lawn with your water hose.

A selector switch, which determined the rate of fire, could be set at 2,000 or 4,000 shots per minute per gun. It also allowed the gunner to select either right, left, or both guns. Once the trigger was depressed, an automatic interrupter switch allowed a three-second burst of fire equaling 100 rounds per gun before automatically stopping its operation. The trigger then had to be released and depressed again if the gunner wished to apply additional fire at his target. This was an ammunition-saving device, as each gun only had 3,000 rounds before requiring reloading.

The AC then showed me the seven-shot rocket pods on either side of the aircraft, their attaching points, and interface cables. He also showed me the selector switch on the dash panel between our seats, called an intervalometer, which would determine the number of rockets to be fired each time he depressed his fire switch located on his cyclic control. Each 2.75-inch rocket had a new seventeen-pound warhead, each producing 21,000 pieces of shrapnel equaling the same impact as a 105 mm howitzer cannon round.

This day, our light-fire team of two gunships was on standby down in the gun shack. Once the briefings were over and aircraft were pre-flighted, fueled, and ready to go, the gun shack was our 'ready room.' It was only about fifty yards from our parked choppers. The hut contained one pair of bunk beds, several chairs with a table, and one shelf of the same old books everyone else had read for the last two or three years.

The one thing I didn't like about the gun shack was the PRC-45 FM (Prick 45) radio that was used for the operations room to launch our 'gun' teams. The only way we would know we were being called was to have the squelch on. Anyone around one of these radios with squelch on knew what that crazy white noise sounded like. We couldn't turn the volume down too low or we would never hear a radio call. Hence, a loud hissing sound prevailed throughout the small shack.

This morning, it didn't take long for the call to come through,

"Gladiators, launch! We'll give you the coordinates on departure!"

I will never forget the first ride I had as a co-pilot in a UH-1B Huey gunship. We all exploded through the door and ran to our ships as fast as we could. The crew chief untied the main rotor blades while we were strapping into our bulletproof seats. All the switches were preset, so all I had to do was turn on the battery switch and hit the start button while the aircraft commander was strapping in. When his seat belt was secured, the AC took over while I buckled in. The two crewmen in the back had already put their monkey straps on, attaching them to the aircraft in the event they fell out. I timed this scramble exercise one day, and we were off the ground in less than one minute! That's pretty impressive.

Even though I had three months of flying with the company, I was incredibly excited to finally experience the adrenaline-fueled experience of flying an attack helicopter. However, the one thing I always remembered during our departure was, *You play the game, you take your chances,* as we went through the translational lift.

Because the aircraft was always fully loaded, the AC only came up to about a two-inch hover, careful not to spill any lift as we backed out of our revetment.

"Spartan Tower, Gladiator 31 flight of two, request departure."

"Gladiator 31, Spartan Tower, winds 310 at 05, altimeter setting 29.95, cleared for departure to the west."

By the time this radio chatter had finished, we had already passed through translational lift and, as usual, were struggling to gain any altitude because of our heavy load. As we continued climbing, the hog ship was right behind us. Just as we passed through a height of approximately 100 feet, our company operations officer was on the UHF radio.

"Spartan 31, ready to copy?"

"31, go ahead," I replied.

"Roger, 31," the voice was calm and authoritative, giving us the tactical six-digit coordinates for north and east, "Contact call sign is Bravo 26 on frequency 62.7"—FM radio—"They are in a heavy firefight with approximately one platoon of VC and suggest you make your approach from the southwest to their location."

"Gladiator 31, roger copy," replied 31.

As this was being said, I was madly writing with my grease pencil on the windshield, making sure of call signs, radio frequencies, and coordinates.

With the tactical map in my lap, the minute I plotted the coordinates, I called out to the AC. "Pick up a heading of 080 degrees. We should be there in about twelve minutes."

Now it was my turn to get busy.

"Saigon arty, Saigon arty, Gladiator 31, Bien Hoa to (our assigned coordinates)."

"Gladiator 31, Saigon arty, Fire Support Base Jane firing on a heading of 200 degrees, 16,000 feet; Fire Support Base Diane firing on a heading of 050 degrees, 18,000 feet. How do you copy?"

"Saigon arty, 31, roger, Fire Support Base Mary and Diane, roger copy," came my reply.

After finishing that last radio transmission, I studied the map briefly, mentally plotting the azimuth and altitude. We were well clear of the artillery fire. I peeled my eyes off the map and scanned the panel before me. We climbed to 1,500 feet on a heading of 80 degrees. I saw that the heading would be slightly to the southwest of our intended infantry unit and instructed the AC to turn right approximately 10 degrees for a heading correction.

"Show me the map," he said.

Because I was brand new to the gun platoon, I wasn't the least surprised he wanted to look at my track on the map and verify exactly what I said. I knew this would be done several times before he was comfortable with my capabilities. By now, we were only about five minutes out.

"Go guns hot, select one rocket," he then said.

As co-pilot, part of my job was to mind the overhead circuit breaker panel and set the rocket selector switch, determining the number of rockets fired with each press of the fire button on the AC cyclic control. Because we always pulled the circuit breakers on the final approach at the end of the day, it was also routine to push them back in before engagement; otherwise, nothing worked!

Things were happening at a faster pace now.

He instructed me, "Dial in the frequency and set my radio selector switch to 1," which was the FM radio.

I did as requested. "His call sign is Bravo 26."

"Thanks," he answered. "Bravo 26, Gladiator 31."

Dave was on his third consecutive tour flying gunships for the 190th. He was self-assured and confident, and always kept a cool head. I admired and respected him greatly.

"Gladiator 31, Bravo 26, go ahead." The six in is callsign designated him as the commanding officer of whatever size unit he was in control of.

"Bravo 26, we're approximately two to three mikes"—minutes— "out. Pop smoke, what's your situation?"

The weather had been deteriorating while we were inbound, and the ceiling was now about twenty feet above the jungle canopy. This meant that tactically we had to get down virtually skids in the trees while maintaining our eighty knots of airspeed.

We were able to use the thick jungle for cover while flying low-level in several ways. Firstly, it was terribly difficult to tell from which direction we were approaching. Secondly, because the line of sight was so uncertain, even if the enemy saw us flash past, he wouldn't have time to get his weapon up for an accurate shot. This also kept our noise footprint in a much smaller circle. Occasionally, this would allow us a slight element of surprise while working over heavy jungle.

Because Dave had instructed Bravo 26 to 'pop smoke,' the crew's eyes were straining to see colored smoke rise above the bright green jungle canopy. It always seemed to take forever for this to occur. All of us were scanning our field of view, waiting to see the brightly colored stain wafting up through the canopy. We took up a racetrack pattern around the area about a mile to the southwest of our intersecting coordinates on the map.

Another thing to keep in mind when we asked for a unit to 'pop smoke' was to mention no colors. This was a precautionary measure if the enemy were on the same FM radio frequency. We would have to continue to orbit until we finally saw smoke rising from the jungle and call the infantry, stating the color of the smoke that we could see.

The VC learned early in the game to carry US smoke grenades they had liberated, in the usual colors of red, yellow, purple, green, and white. I might have seen up to three different colors of smoke at different nearby locations simultaneously when we asked a unit to pop smoke. Luckily, the colors would be different each time, or we would have to request another smoke grenade.

Several of us spotted the smoke at the same time.

"Bravo 26, I see banana," said Dave, referring to yellow smoke.

"Roger that, Gladiator, on a heading of 080 from my smoke 60 meters. The enemy is dug into several bunkers."

"Roger, 26, I'll make my approach from the southwest."

Please keep in mind that the hog ship had always been above and behind us. When the cloud was low, they flew as high as they could off to one side, so as not to fly the same flight path we were on, once we knew where the enemy was located. The additional height was necessary for the maximum-accuracy angular delivery of the rockets. Because the minigun ship was always lower, it provided us a great deal of protection through firepower, should we get into trouble from below. The hog ship carried nineteen pairs of rockets, which made them equal to a battery of 38 X 105 mm howitzer cannon rounds. They did not have externally mounted miniguns like we did, but their door gunners were extremely efficient, and each had a minimum of 2,000 rounds of machine-gun ammunition.

Now that we had established radio contact with the infantry and knew their exact location, and that of the enemy, we began setting up a racetrack attack pattern. This pattern is exactly as it sounds: an oval pattern with its main axis being the attack leg. We would then dive while releasing rockets and 'hosing' the area with the minigun.

One of our golden rules while engaging was 'never overfly the target.' We would perform a hard right (or left) climbing break at a distance of approximately 200 to 300 meters prior to overflying the target. The theory behind this attack pattern was that each time the lower aircraft would break from engagement, his wingmen would roll in exactly at that time, laying down a heavy stream of rockets and machine-gun fire, consequently keeping the enemy's head down.

Dave was briefing me for our first run on the target, "Put your minigun on my rocket burst, nowhere else!"

Now the adrenaline was really pumping! We were still flying about twenty feet above the treetops with our skids almost in the trees.

The door gunner and crew chief were locked and cocked, each of them hanging out of their doors, with their M-60s suspended on strong rubber bungee cords and a smoke grenade held in either hand, with pins pulled. If they spotted anything or took fire, all they had to do was drop the grenade and return fire, and this made locating the enemy far easier in the undulating jungle canopy.

Now we were skimming across the top of the rainforest, tracking for an inbound leg in an oval racetrack flight pattern, and suddenly, what must have been a full magazine of thirty rounds from an AK-47 exploded past our aircraft on full automatic. It was a long burst on the right-hand side of the aircraft, and the sonic boom from the high-powered bullets whizzing past us was deafening!

"Smokes out!" shouted the door gunner while he sprayed the area the sound came from with machine-gun fire.

We were still over 500 yards from our infantry and must have stumbled onto another unit of VC.

However, our first obligation was to our assigned infantry, so we left our smoke grenade to do its job and did a slow break to our right, continuing to climb approximately forty feet, putting our main rotor in the clouds. We tracked overhead our own infantry on a heading of eighty degrees, releasing a few rockets at sixty meters from the now rapidly disappearing smoke cloud, and breaking rapidly to our right to not overfly the target.

As soon as our rockets hit the treetops, our door gunners opened up, and I poured the minigun fire into that area for a quick three-second burst. I'm sure this would have kept the enemy's heads down for that immediate critical moment when the belly of our aircraft was facing them. The door gunners were desperately hanging out with one foot on the skid and one foot on the floor, firing between their legs, continuing to protect our vulnerable position as we continued our break, climbing right in a rather flat ninety-degree bank.

Dave was now pulling maximum power and rolling out of the break, leveling out into a slight climb, allowing him to get to the position to dive inboard behind the hog ship before he started his break after its rocket run. The low altitude forced us to change our tactics to meet the situation, and that wasn't easy.

As we were scrambling to reach the point to turn inbound for our run covering the hog ship, I looked over my right shoulder, watching the impact from its rockets exploding in the treetops. With the final explosion from 23's rocket run, I saw a black-clad man come cartwheeling out of the top of a very tall tree.

I yelled at Dave, "I just saw VC falling out of the top of that tree! He's wearing black pajamas!"

"Are you sure?" asked Dave.

"Yes, definitely!" came my reply.

"Put me up, VHF," David said.

I rotated his radio selector switch from 1 to 2 (from FM to VHF radio).

"38, 38," called Dave.

"38, go ahead."

"Roger, my co-pilot says he saw VC falling out of one of the trees you just shot up. I guess that gives you a kill!"

"Roger that, 31!" replied Gladiator 38.

You could hear the smile in his voice.

By now, we were reaching the outbound portion of our run. I could see Dave looking back at 38, judging when to turn inbound in time to protect his wingman's break. Only a few seconds later, Dave broke hard just as 38 started his break. He leveled our ship, and the M-60s from the door gunners began hammering the target area, hopefully keeping the enemy's heads down. Dave pumped two more rockets as I poured in the minigun's deadly stream of red tracers.

Our door gunners continued firing as we started our break. The right gunner was still standing with one foot on the skid and one still on the floor of the aircraft. This allowed him to continue firing, covering our break.

It's worth noting that a door gunner had slipped from this position more than once while firing, consequently hitting the back of the ACs bulletproof seat two or three times before he could get his finger off the trigger. The reaction to such a 'slipup' was, without fail, one very angry AC! He would usually wind up giving the door gunner a real piece of his mind, either immediately after or when we landed to rearm and refuel.

We continued the racetrack attack until the infantry called on FM, "Gladiator, cease fire! I reckon you guys have nailed them; we're going in to look."

"Roger, Bravo 36. We took some fire about a kilometer to our east. We're going over to see if we can stir them up."

We proceeded to the area that was marked by only a waft of smoke and did several sweeps through the area at low level, skids almost touching the tops of the jungle. We slowed down to sixty knots but still couldn't draw any fire. I believe they had some idea of what we had just done to their comrades and weren't up for the game, so to speak.

As we picked up the heading for Bien Hoa, Dave keyed his mic, "Hey, 31, Guay lost his cherry today!"

He smiled into his mic. Well, I guess I did, and what a ride it was for me!

22

FIND THAT .51 CAL.

.51-caliber heavy machine gun. Drawing by Katherine Nielsen.

One day, in particular, I wasn't rostered to fly. It was hot and sticky, and around the 0800 mark, I went over to the mess hall, had a late breakfast, returned to the room, and tidied up.

Our gun platoon was on standby/scramble to work with any infantry unit requirements in the local area of operations, so two gunships were already pre-flighted with their crews in the gun shack next to the flight line and ready to launch. The other gunships had already departed with the slicks for the day's missions. Hence, I scored a well-deserved day off because I was high on flight time for the month. For those of you who might be interested, we didn't go by the number of days in a row we had flown. Instead, our cumulative flight time had a limit of 140 hours in a running thirty-day total. This was how we determined when we had a day off.

I had elected to relax and read a book, so with my feet up in my bunk and not much to do, I was chilling out and enjoying myself. The room's air conditioner was working like a charm. That all wasn't going to last long. There was a sudden, rather urgent knocking on my door.

"Come in," I called out.

It was a crew chief from one of the slick aircraft that hadn't been used for the day.

"Good morning, Mr. Guay," he said with a concerned look. "Captain Hun is up at flight ops and he'd like you to come up ASAP."

"Do you know what this is about?" I asked.

"Not really, sir, something about a .51 cal. and a Navy ammunition barge not far from here."

"Thanks, chief," I replied as he exited the door.

I pivoted on my bunk and quickly laced my boots up. As in most cases having anything to do with aviation, it was always a long walk to get anywhere. I set off quickly and headed toward flight ops (operations), adjacent to our hover lanes on the flight line.

As I walked into flight ops, I didn't get the usual big batch of smiles from most of the staff. They were all REMFs (rear echelon mother fuckers), almost a term of endearment for the admin staff who ran the show twenty-four hours a day. Captain Hun, my platoon commander, was leaning over the operations officer's desk, having a low-volume chat. When he saw me enter, he straightened up, facing me, and folded his arms. He was about my height and had black hair and a body like a tree trunk. The captain was a good-natured person but wasn't in a smiling mood at that moment.

"Mr. Guay, we have a rather unusual situation," he said as I walked up. "The only gunship available now is red-Xed." Red-Xed is a term used to describe an unflyable aircraft with a maintenance issue. He continued, "A Navy 155-millimeter ammunition barge has been ambushed not far from here on the Dong Nai River, and the battalion wants us to find the .51 cal. and neutralize it. Because you are the only pilot in the gun platoon who is still current in flight time in a slick, I want you to take one and find this .51 cal."

You could have knocked me over with a feather. Immediately, my heart started racing, and I found myself panting slightly, imagining the worst. A .51-caliber is a magnificent anti-aircraft heavy machine gun with a maximum effective range of 2,400 meters, or almost 8,000 feet. It fires 600 rounds per minute, and would go through almost one inch of steel armor plating at 500 meters, or 1,600 feet, like hot butter. Of course, anything else that got in its way would be shredded, including myself, any other crew member, or the turbine engine.

"Yes, sir," I replied.

The operations manager gave me a tail number for the Huey I was to use and told me that the crew was already there. I asked him if he would mind if I could choose some extra crew members to man two additional M-60s from his operations staff, to which he had no objections.

Of course, all the administrative staff in operations, which totaled six personnel, had listened to every word we were saying.

I looked around the room and said loudly, "Would anyone like to come along for a ride in a Huey with an M-60 and 2,000 rounds of ammo?"

All the hands went up! I chose three men who looked pretty switched on.

"Follow me to the armorer, and we'll pick up weapons for the two of you."

I selected the third clerk to sit in the front seat as ballast for center of gravity purposes. None of us had done this before, but they knew they were in for an adventure!

I wasn't about to go after the enemy's number one anti-aircraft gun and crew without being armed as heavily as possible. I didn't know any of these soldiers, but if they were brave enough to come along, that was good enough for me.

As we walked out of operations and to the nearest hangar where the armory was located, I sighted two slick door gunners I had recognized that weren't working for the day.

"Good afternoon, gentlemen. Would you both be interested in coming with me on number 236? I'm taking six door gunners, and we'll be searching for a .51 cal. along the Dong Nai about ten miles from here."

They looked at each other briefly, shrugged their shoulders, and said, "Sure, why not?"

The five of us walked into the armory. The armory sergeant, on his second tour, knew the ropes very well.

"Sergeant, could you please supply us with four M-60s and 2,000 rounds each? We've been tasked with finding a .51 cal. along the Dong Nai not far from here."

The sergeant's eyes widened a little, realizing the gravity of our assignment. With a quiet smile, he said, "Certainly, sir."

"Thank you," I replied.

I turned and looked at the four gunners and said, "I'll see you at the aircraft."

As I walked out to the assigned chopper, I was pleased to find a crew chief I had known very well for a while. He and the door gunner already had their weapons armed and ready to go.

"Chief, are we ready to go?"

"Yes, sir, I finished the pre-flight twenty minutes ago. We've got 1,000 pounds of fuel."

I started walking around the aircraft, looking in the engine deck inspection doors, checking the fuel cap, jumping onto the tail rotor stinger for a quick check of the tail rotor, rounding the other side to check the engine inspection doors, then climbed up the side of the Huey, had a feel of the main rotor bearings, a quick look at the various push-pull tubes and connectors, the swashplate—all were good. I was satisfied the aircraft was in solid shape.

About this time, the additional four gunners arrived. They were speaking among themselves in rather excited banter. As they approached, I called them over and addressed the seven of them.

"I want to have two of you sitting on the floor on either side of the aircraft with your ammo cans next to you, with ammo feeding from the left. The crew chief will show you where to put the ammo can and how to feed the ammunition to your M-60. When we get out over the river, I will instruct you to test your weapons. Just fire enough rounds into the river to ensure you are happy your machine gun is functioning correctly. For Christ's sake, don't shoot the skids!"

Then I addressed the extra clerk.

"You sit in the right seat to keep my weight and balance correct. Don't touch anything, and just enjoy the ride. If you have any questions, feel free to ask. When we reach the search area, I'll be coming in low. We've got to spread the nipa palm apart and find what we can find. If we find anything at all, trust your judgment, but shoot first and ask questions later. Are there any questions?"

I studied their faces, but they all seemed confident in my instructions with no questions.

"Okay, let's get this show on the road."

Each crewman had a helmet on and hooked into the intercom. At the same time, they loaded up as instructed, with the door gunner and crew chief mounted behind their already prepared M-60 machine guns mounted on sissy sticks.

The M-60 machine gun fires approximately 600 7.62 mm bullets, or rounds, per minute. Our platoon gunners knew a few tricks and fine-tuned them to about 800 rounds a minute. Because of our task, I purposefully enlisted the help of six gunners, ready to fire 4,800 rounds a minute should we encounter any hostile activity.

I started the aircraft, listening to the reassuring *tick, tick, tick* of the two igniter plugs in the turbine engine, while the engine rpm advanced toward the green arc on the N1 gauge (engine rpm in percentage), with the exhaust gas temperature (EGT) gauge staying in the green. Turning around and checking the crew on both sides, I got the thumbs-up from everyone.

"Spartan Tower, Spartan 286 Coliseum, ready for takeoff."

"Spartan 286, Spartan Tower. Altimeter 3002, winds are light and variable, lane 1 departure is clear."

"Spartan 936, roger."

"Coming up," I said to the crew via the intercom.

"Clear up back and right," "Clear up back and left," came the routine replies from the crew chief and door gunner.

Parked in our L-shaped revetments, we were required to hover backward, all the way to the centerline of our lane, clearing the large steel protective shields that helped protect our Hueys from rocket attacks, even though they were only five feet high. When I could see the long white line coming into my field of vision from the left, I did a pedal turn. I centered the Huey over the lane centerline, maintaining a height of about three feet above the asphalt. I did a quick hover check, observing the torque I was pulling, the rotor tach, the amount of fuel aboard, and all my temperature and pressure gauges. Everything looked good. This check only took a few seconds.

"Spartan Tower, 286 ready for takeoff."

"Roger, 286, cleared for takeoff."

US Navy ammunition barge with a cargo of 155 mm howitzer rounds. Photo supplied by Patrick Mullen, Spartan 12 and Stogie 13.

Glancing at the torque gauge, I began the slow hover forward to translational lift. As the nose of the aircraft took a slight dip, we started to accelerate and climb out. I performed my usual ritual, thinking out loud, "You play the game, you take your chances." We continued climbing as I banked to the right toward the Dong Nai River, which was not far. I climbed to an altitude of 500 feet en route, picked up my 80 knots of airspeed, and leveled off, tracking toward the six-digit coordinate block on the map that I had been given as the location for the attack.

The Dong Nai River was almost half a mile wide as we began to fly over its main body. Now that I was away from civilization, I dropped to an altitude of fifty feet and flew straight up the middle of the river.

"All right, everybody, test your weapons."

I never got used to the sudden deafening explosions from the muzzle of these weapons. Especially now, with over 4,000 bullets a minute going into the river, it was bloody amazing.

"Cease fire!" I shouted into the intercom.

Everyone stopped firing, and I believe they were buzzing a little from the adrenaline that had just been injected into their systems. It would be about a five-minute leg to get to the ambush site. When I sighted the area that matched the coordinates, I turned and tracked straight to it.

"Get on your guns! Get ready!" I called into the intercom.

I then dropped to an altitude of ten feet above the tops of the nipa palm, maintaining my eighty knots, which lowered my noise footprint while approaching the target area.

I quickly lifted the aircraft nose and reduced my collective, then as I got within about fifty feet of the intended hover point, I let the momentum of the maneuver carry the Huey toward it. I settled the aircraft to an almost level attitude and pulled in a large amount of pitch as I dropped the nose, stopping my forward motion and creating a massive downward wind, blowing a large area of nipa apart. I maintained my fifteen-foot hover, spreading the clumps of their perfectly formed upward-reaching deep-green fronds, some standing as much as fifteen feet high, completely flat. Doing this would expose anything hiding behind or underneath its canopy. Now, everyone on the ship was wired, their eyes peeled for anything unusual. Everyone was looking for a target. I would hover left for a while, slide right, then left, and right, continuing the search. We all knew that if we found what we were looking for, we were in huge trouble. I would fly forward about the length of the aircraft and then start hovering to the left and right again, and again, exposing the three machine guns on the approach side, and having the other 3 guns covering our retreating side. Nothing so far—thank God for that.

We continued this search method for about fifteen minutes, covering a relatively large area. We were looking for a five-foot-long heavy machine gun, most likely carried by two or three men and set up in a camouflaged position. By the time we arrived, the gun could have been moved anywhere, with the ample time frame of approximately forty-five minutes. Nevertheless, we continued to search along the river's edge and inland for approximately 500 meters along the bank, north and south of the coordinates.

The VC had escaped, precisely as they planned. During our search, hardly a word had been spoken, keeping a clear channel on the intercom should something happen.

"How would you guys like to go to a free-fire zone near here and burn up some ammo?"

A very quick loud-and-clear "Yes, sir!" came through the intercom.

"Blue Boy, Blue Boy, Spartan 286," I called naval operations for the local district on the FM radio.

"Spartan 286, Blue Boy, go ahead."

"Blue Boy, negative sighting of any possible target in the search area, Spartan 286 request entry to free fire zone Delta Bravo for approximately one-zero minutes."

"Roger, Spartan 286, you are cleared Delta Bravo advise upon zone exit."

"286, roger."

Now, it was time for the fun to start. I took a heading crossing the river. We would arrive there in approximately four minutes, just enough time for a briefing.

In the way of explanation, a free-fire zone is precisely that: there should be no friendly troops or civilians in this area. Everything else is a target. I had been there several times and knew its boundaries.

"Okay, listen up. I'll let you know when we get to the free-fire zone. Wait for my command to commence firing. Keep your impact zone within 50 to 600 meters of the aircraft. Don't melt your barrels—if they go white, cease firing, or they will bend. If for any reason I want you to stop firing, I will call cease-fire, cease-fire, cease-fire. We are about two minutes out."

As we crossed the boundary not far from the opposite side of the river, I shouted into the intercom, "Commence firing!"

With that command, all hell broke loose. As I flew a wide circle, the tracers were going everywhere. It's hard to explain the power a person feels when firing such a deadly and effective weapon on fully automatic. The adrenaline starts pumping, your attention is laser-focused, and you have the power of life and death in your hands. It didn't take long for the ammunition to be fully expended. It was easy to tell as silence fell upon the aircraft in place of the ridiculously loud booming from the M-60s. I had timed it reasonably well and had picked up the heading for Bien Hoa as we exited the zone.

"Blue Boy, Spartan 286."

"286, go ahead."

"Roger, 286 has exited the zone."

"Roger, thank you for your assistance today. Better hunting next time."

"Roger that. See you next time," I said.

We were now approaching the Spartan landing area at Bien Hoa. "Spartan Tower, Spartan 286," I called.

"Spartan 286, Spartan Tower, go ahead."

"Spartan Tower, Spartan 286 is inbound currently NDB Mountain." Non-Directional Beacon Mountain was a small hill in the otherwise perfectly flat landscape, used as a position reporting point for approaching the Coliseum. "Gear down and welded."

The phrase was a standing joke each time the slicks came in for landing.

"Roger, 286, I've got you in sight. You are cleared to land," said the tower controller.

"Spartan 286, roger," was my reply.

Now, the banter inside the ship picked up rapidly, and everyone was still buzzed up from firing off their ammo, happy to be home. You could feel the relief within the crew that this exercise was over. I hovered down the laneway to my original parking spot, landed, and continued to shut the aircraft down as all the crewmen recovered their empty ammo boxes and M-60s and made their way to the armory to clean their weapons. They were all smiling and gave me winks, nods, and thumbs-up signs as they walked past. I knew I would have no trouble the next time this kind of mission came up.

I turned the radio selector switch to UHF and called Spartan operations.

"Spartan operations, Spartan 286. Negative target sighted, and we're shutting down now."

"Roger, 286, will relay your message to the ops officer."

"286," came my final call of the day.

And so ended the mission that had the potential to be an utter disaster. I performed this search twice more before my tour ended. I learned that about two months after my departure, a very good friend flying an OH-58 Kiowa was tasked with the same search. Sadly, he found

Door gunner in UH-1B. Note 'chicken plate' ceramic ballistic laminate in front and back panels.
Photo supplied by Patrick Mullen, Spartan 12 and Stogie 13.

a group of VC in the search area, and before he began engaging them, they fired first. He was killed instantly, his door gunner wounded. Rest in peace, Warrant Officer 1 Patrick Fitzsimmons. You were a true gentleman and a great friend.

23

THE EIGHTEEN ELEPHANTS

Warning: This story is brutal. It was suggested I omit it, but I feel it is one way to display the insanity of war. If you are faint of heart, please just skip to the next story. Read it if you choose, but you have been warned. Sadly, it is another true story that still haunts me to this day.

Our wake-up time was 0500. We had been told the previous evening that we were to do a reconnaissance flight in War Zone D in the morning. This was a notoriously dangerous area of high enemy activity. I was to fly co-pilot in the minigun ship. However, this was no ordinary recon flight. We were told that there were 2,000 VC and NVA in the area we were to reconnoiter, and that we would be going out as a heavy-fire team of three gunships. Well, at least we would have the firepower to respond in kind to any groundfire we might take.

Let's see, a team of three gunships, assuming two minigun ships and one hog, carried a total of 24,000 rounds of 7.62 machine-gun ammo and 66 X 2.75-inch folding fin aerial rockets, each with the impact of a 105 mm howitzer cannon round.

I had a hearty breakfast, then went back to the room, strapped on my .38-caliber pistol, grabbed my helmet and chicken plate, and made my way to the flight line for the daily aircraft inspection. Hardly a thought was given to our mission, as I preferred just to let things play out in real time. I helped with rearming the minigun system, the most labor-intensive task before takeoff; 3,000 rounds of linked ammunition per minigun were loaded into small trays, which had to be done in a precise manner in order to avoid jamming the weapons. The fourteen seventeen-pound warhead rockets were being loaded at the same time by the crew chief while the door gunner and I completed arming the minis. The last exercise was loading the first round of the linked 7.62 mm bullets into each minigun without accidentally firing a round while you rotated the barrels.

Author helping load 6,000 rounds of 7.62 mm ammunition for miniguns. Photo supplied by Author.

As we approached the coordinates, at an altitude of 5,000 feet, with the C & C ship approximately 1,000 feet above us, we found a huge open field of about five acres, with beautiful emerald green grass and small trees around its borders, gradually merging into heavy jungle. It was a scene of absolute tranquility. As we got nearer the open area, we increased our airspeed from 80 knots to approximately 100 knots while maintaining our altitude. We hoped that this would throw off any potential heavy machine-gun aim by screwing up their necessary lead while they attempted to set their sights on our aircraft.

Each of us was well separated from the other in a kind of loose right echelon formation. We sped across the center of the area, waiting to take fire and, at the same time, observing any unusual features, such as bunkers or signs of disturbance in the grass that might indicate trenches, walking tracks, or other marks on the smooth surface. From this altitude, we couldn't see anything of note.

We were all straining our eyes like crazy, expecting the worst. The door gunners were leaning well out of the ship, constantly scanning, looking for any bright muzzle flashes or arcs of tracer bullets coming up from the jungle. We were speaking to each other on our gunship-to-gunship VHF radio, flying in a wide circular arc, waiting for the inevitable.

A voice came over the VHF. "Are those water buffalo down there?"

We all could see several large animals moving around through the open fields.

"Could be. Kind of hard to tell from way up here."

"They're pachyderms!" came another voice.

"What the hell is a pachyderm?" asked another voice.

"Elephants! They're elephants!"

Holy shit, none of us had ever seen elephants in Vietnam. Of course, those in the C & C ship were listening to us and probably got a shock similar to ours, or perhaps already knew this.

"Gladiator flight, let's go down to 3,000 feet," said 31.

We simply followed the lead gunship down through his descent. Now we were looking for trigger-happy large-caliber weaponry that might be waiting for us. We flew in a slow circular pattern, still no movement of any troops or anything sighted to indicate their presence, except for the elephants.

"Gladiators, let's drop down to 2,000."

Again we followed the lead gunship, down to 2,000. The tension was really ratcheting up now. If there were any .51-caliber heavy machine guns, we would be minced before they could be knocked out. Still no action or motion.

At this altitude, it was much easier to see these four-legged giants as they roamed around, grazing in the heavily grassed area.

"Gladiator 31, C & C."

"C & C, Gladiator 31, go ahead."

"31, C & C, my counterpart"—the South Vietnamese Army representative of equal rank to the American officer in control of this mission—"says all the elephants have to be killed. They're the NVA heavy trucks."

The mission commander told us that these animals had been used to transport large, heavy loads for this massive troop movement. They were the equivalent of the US Army's two-and-a-half-ton truck.

I couldn't believe what I was hearing. I got a huge knot in my stomach. These beautiful creatures were about to be slaughtered through no fault of their own. At first, it was hard for me to get my head around this order, but in the end, it was an order.

Please keep in mind we had drawn no fire yet and were within range of any weapon the enemy might have now, so we chose to begin our attack at a low altitude.

"Gladiator 31, do not, I repeat, do not use rockets. We don't want to start fires down there for incoming slicks."

"Roger, C & C," said Gladiator 31.

Now, our job became much harder. As Gladiator 31 started his descent to begin the execution of these regal beasts, the loud popping noise made by our main rotors while losing altitude frightened them. They immediately started charging from their positions in the open field into the surrounding jungle. The one geographical feature working against them was that they all charged into a large finger of jungle, which protruded into the clearing and finally came to a point. When we saw this happening, all three gunships swooped down lower, which truly panicked the elephants.

"Commence firing!" commanded Dave.

With that, our door gunners started firing, their high-powered M-60 machine-gun bullets striking the elephants randomly, kind of willy-nilly.

"They're not falling!" said the crew chief.

I watched him shooting from our position fifty feet above one enormous bull elephant.

"Concentrate on the spinal column!" a voice came over the radio. After a few seconds of heavy fire, the old bull finally dropped. Now, the elephants were disappearing rapidly into the finger of the jungle pointing toward the center of the large cleared acreage, concentrating them into the small isthmus.

"I can't see any of them through the treetops!" yelled the door gunner.

"Use frags!" More instructions came over the VHF radio, referencing fragmentation grenades. "Drop them in the center of the tree line out toward the edge of the jungle, and scare them out into the clearing."

This was done often in gunships, using hand grenades for different purposes. With no instruction, Dave turned slowly and flew into the center of the finger of the jungle, slowing his airspeed while tracking toward the end of the finger. The rest of us were busy yanking the pins from our grenades and dropping them out of our doors as we flew straight up the center of the large finger of the jungle. Now, we had descended to about twenty feet above the tree line, allowing the grenades to reach the ground before they exploded. This caused maximum panic among the elephants. The violent sound of these explosions worked exactly as planned, with all the elephants scrambling madly out of the cover of the jungle back into the clearing.

Now, the real carnage began. It's one of the most horrible things I've ever seen. Our door gunners would work on one elephant until it fell, but then other nearby elephants would stop running, turn around, and surround the fallen elephant, pushing it with their heads and trying to lift it back onto its feet.

I looked across the massive field and watched the other two gunships, white puffs of smoke rapidly exiting the end of their machine guns, the tracers striking these beautiful animals until they dropped.

I realized these were families, as the same thing happened in small groups across the open field. No matter the size of the fallen elephant, a group of two or three others close by would stop immediately, return to the wounded animal, and try to get it back onto its feet.

They were desperately trying to stand it up. Once they started this task, they wouldn't leave the fallen beast. Sadly, they just became more grist for the mill. We continued to circle the group until they all dropped, then flew to the nearest one we could find, riddling these beautiful, intelligent, majestic animals full of lead. I'm writing this through my tears. It was like firing into a bus load of children.[1] Even telling the story again gives me a horrible knot in my stomach, and tears come to my eyes as I play the whole scene again in my head. Not a good day.

When we finished the slaughter, we all flew around the perimeter of the jungle again, at low level, looking to see if we could find any more victims. Other than the eighteen dead beasts, nothing was visible. Then a call came in from C & C.

"Gladiators, we want you to recon the entire area bordered by the jungle and half a click"—half a kilometer—"into the canopy as well. You're cleared to recon by fire."

With that, all three gunships did as ordered. We shot everything that looked even a little suspicious, a small mound of earth, fallen logs that might look like a bunker firing slit. We fired up the jungle and the peninsula that came out into the clearing with the M-60s. The other two gunships were working the perimeter and half a kilometer into the jungle and its surrounding area, shooting at anything that did or didn't move. What we were trying to do was to draw fire from anywhere. If they shot at us, we could see them.

This continued for fifteen minutes until we were low on fuel.

"C & C, Gladiator 31."

"31, go ahead," replied C & C.

"Roger, we're getting low on fuel."

"Roger, 31, looks like we are going to change plans here. You can RTB"—return to base.

"Roger, C & C."

"Gladiators, RTB," 31 said.

---

[1] While all of this killing was going on, there was no malice, no mental aggression, none of the things we usually felt when we were required to kill another human. It was killing for the sake of killing. In my opinion, that's the worst kind.

With that command, we all turned and headed for Bien Hoa. That was the end of the day's action for us. I believe that, collectively, we were all in various states of shock after having killed such highly revered animals so indiscriminately. It's one of those terrible things you never forget.

That night, back at the O Club (Officers Club), where we often shared a table or chatted at the bar with a few drinks, not a word was spoken about our mission that day. I'm certain that to this day, we are all still affected one way or another whenever we think about it.

The next morning, I think we were all quite surprised when, shortly after our pre-flight inspections were completed, our heavy-fire team from the previous day was ordered to return to the same location for another VR (visual reconnaissance). By the time the orders came through, we were fully rearmed and refueled, ready to go.

The flight time to this area was approximately thirty minutes, which did not seem very long under the circumstances. Once again, thinking back, as our minds wandered en route, we realized that our three ships were going to fly straight back into what could be a maelstrom of heavy fire from a huge number of troops. No one mentioned this, but the lid had been removed from a case of fragmentation grenades, and all weapons were locked and cocked as we approached the area.

As we approached from 5,000 feet, we could see that C & C was overhead again. "Gladiator 31, C & C."

"C & C, Gladiator 31, go ahead."

"Roger, Gladiator, we want you to do a thorough recon again through this area. Use recon by fire."

"Roger," came the reply.

This again meant firing at any potential or suspected location, bunker slot, or anywhere the door gunners suspected was a potential location for the enemy to hide. The idea was to make the enemy think he had been spotted if the rounds impacted close enough to his location, and encourage him to shoot back. It was often used to look for absolutely anything and everything that might show troop movements or the enemy, throughout the entire location.

Once again, we flew over the area at 5,000 feet, then dropped to 2,000, and still no fire was taken from any direction. Once we had satisfied ourselves that not even small arms were going to open up on us, we went in for a very close look at about 100 knots and 50 feet. The door gunner and crew chief were ready with M-60s and didn't require any further instructions. They were hammering everything as we zipped around for the first five minutes.

The tracers were zinging all over the place. No return fire. Dammit. We slowed down to eighty knots, our usual cruise speed, still fifty feet off the ground, buzzing around at high speed like bluebottle flies, still no incoming fire. I didn't feel the necessity to use the miniguns without a hard target. We were all over the place in this large area, at least two square kilometers of open space.

The crew chief on this day had a rather twisted sense of humor and got up to a bit of mischief.

He was firing long, sustained bursts from his machine gun. Suddenly, I could hear a rapid *ting, ting, ting, ting* on the back of my helmet and realized it was the spent hot brass being discharged from his M-60, going straight down the back of my shirt. Shit, it was hot!

I turned around to find him grinning broadly, not looking where he was shooting but watching where the hot brass was going. He was feeding it in a constant arc off the back of my helmet and inside my collar!

I grinned back at him and yelled at the top of my voice, "Cease fire!"

The brass just kept coming.

"Cease fire! That's an order!"

He was still grinning at me as he released his finger from the trigger. That's the first and only time I ever used that phrase I heard in the movies, "That's an order!"

I think the entire crew was surprised when I said it, and it was a moment of great levity.

I had already quickly pulled the tail of my shirt out, allowing the freshly fired red-hot brass to fall onto the floor while it was still painting my back in red stripes.

We all had fun in our different ways. I quickly learned that until I was an aircraft commander in the gunships, I would be fair game for any pranks from the crew. It was a great way to break the boredom and stress.

Our three gunships flew around for approximately half an hour, shooting everything in sight. We called it recon by fire but were still unable to use rockets. We couldn't find anything suspicious, nothing at all—except for one thing.

Many of the elephants had had large squares of their skin removed in order to butcher the meat that lay beneath. *They were being butchered to feed the masses.* Holy smoke! Well, at least they didn't go to waste completely.

Because of the emotional toll the previous day took on all of us, I'm sure we were all very pleased there were no more to be found on that second day.

It just goes to show you that when an enemy wants to hide properly, even on a large scale, it can be done. We knew they were there, and after we finished our second reconnaissance, our unit never returned. I don't know if there ever was a combat assault in that area, and I didn't hear any stories.

24

Warrant Officer 1 Michael Hatfield. Photo supplied by 190th AHC.
His friendship was as big as his smile.

THE DEATH OF A GOOD FRIEND

M ichael Hatfield joined our company in mid-February 1970. When I met him, he was still feeling the sting of what it was like to be called a fucking new guy (FNG). As I was told early on in my stint when I joined the company and wore the FNG title, "A new guy is the most dangerous weapon the VC have against the United States Army." To me, that statement was like water off a duck's back. But sitting in the right front seat of the Huey as a new co-pilot, it did dawn on me that a) I did not understand the language, b) I could not pronounce the names of any locations in South Vietnam, c) I had no idea where the villages were whose names I could pronounce. Hence, I could understand the sentiment toward a new guy.

One evening, sitting at the bar having my mandatory bourbon Cokes while calming my nerves after a day's work, I looked to my right to see a shiny new green flight suit occupied by a real FNG that I had seen around the company for a few weeks. I had not worked with him because I was then in the gunship platoon, and he was a slick driver.

It was the custom in our unit for the new guys to address senior warrant officers (someone who wasn't an FNG, even if he was the same rank) by his formal title of Mister. It wasn't very often that a senior warrant officer would address an FNG unless he was in an emergency situation. I saw him glance at my nametag from the corner of my eye.

Turning toward him, I said, "How's it goin'?"

Initially, all I got in reply was a wide-eyed 'deer in the headlights' look.

"Ahh, mmm, er, Mr. Guay, good, really good."

The thing about the reply was that he was smiling. That's one thing I did not expect from someone who should be feeling so downtrodden and horribly picked on. I believe that if a person sees someone smile, it is practically a reflex to smile back, which I did. In my book, that smile was a bit of an icebreaker.

"You can drop Mr. Guay. Just call me Richard," I said, and we shook hands.

I wasn't sure how many times he had experienced that greeting, but it would not have been many by this stage. He smiled, then I got the grin, and he said, "Thanks, Richard, I appreciate that."

"I know it's a bit late, but welcome to the company. I think it's probably one of the very best in Vietnam. Don't take anything personally if people are hard on you. It's just the way things get done around here."

Again, he smiled, "I've already figured that out. But I am enjoying the flying, and trying to learn all these stupid names as fast as possible. Calling for arty is pure torture. But I am getting the hang of it."

"The next part isn't just pronouncing the names; it's remembering where all those stupid names are located. Don't worry, a few more weeks and you'll start settling in really well," I replied.

My initial impression was that Michael was one of those 'glass half full' guys. In some ways, it was a breath of fresh air to speak with someone whose inner core was still intact, not shattered yet by heavy combat. From that point on, we really did get on like the proverbial house fire. It was good that I was in a different platoon and not working with him as an aircraft commander. This allowed us to speak without the stilted, businesslike discourse generated by military dictum. We really did get to know each other on a personal level, and under the circumstances, that didn't happen very often.

Michael had this effect on several other more senior warrants. He was just a really likable guy.

As time passed, I noticed he was one of those fellows who had a presence, and once he started relaxing and getting his self-confidence back, Michael made many friends within the unit in a very short time. In my opinion, this was backed up by the fact that he was one of those people who wasn't often addressed as Mike, but in fact, remained Michael.

Three or four weeks later, as our flight returned to Bien Hoa at the end of our mission day, while we were hovering down our respective lanes for parking, operations came up on UHF radio.

"Mr. Hatfield, operations." There was a brief hesitation on the air, as it was very uncommon for anyone to be called by their name on any frequency.

"Operations, Mr. Hatfield," came the reply.

"It is my pleasure to inform you that we have just received a message. Your child has been born, and both mother and baby are healthy and happy. Congratulations!"

If I recall correctly, the baby was a girl. There were two to three minutes full of congratulations for Michael on the frequency. The emotion generated by that sort of news was infectious and made us all feel good.

Several of us pilots spent most of that evening with Michael in the officers club, not necessarily drinking a lot, just talking and laughing. I think we played cards of some sort. It was a really happy time.

The next morning, March 22, 1970, the flight launched to insert quite a few US infantry out to War Zone D, northeast of Xuan Loc. We called it Indian country, not a good place to go. I didn't fly that day because I was high on my thirty-day cumulative hourly flight time total.

It was early evening, and I was in the mess hall having my dinner when one of the other pilots in my platoon came over and told me that Michael had been killed. A rocket-propelled grenade hit his aircraft and ignited the fuel load, killing him instantly. I can't remember who else was killed or wounded by the explosion. I was totally shocked, shattered, angry, and saddened.

I immediately had a flashback to the previous evening, all the laughter, the pride he had exuded, the genuine happiness he had spread among all of us at the table. Goddammit, it made me angry, and at the same time, I felt great sorrow for his wife and new baby.

I had received a similar message only last December while landing at the end of the day and remembered how I had felt then. For many of us, it was the first time anyone in our unit had been killed very soon after the birth of his child. It was quite unnerving if you spent too much time thinking about it.

My thoughts slipped to the effect this was going to have on his wife and family. The empathy I felt saddened me greatly. In my opinion, it was the family, the wives, and the sweethearts that were the heroes of this war. They never knew what was happening to us, while many of us casually went from day to day, not really feeling any responsibility to write a letter and let them know we were okay.

While I was researching this story, I found a tribute to Michael Hatfield on the 190th Assault Helicopter Company website, with the YouTube URL below. I find it very touching, with some of the best photos of our slick aircraft that I've seen on the net. When you have the time, please take four minutes of your life and watch this tribute to a young man who gave his life for his country and was killed in action. Rest in peace, brother.

Michael Hatfield "An Average Day"
By SpartanOneOne YouTube

25

BAR STORY NUMBER TWO: TURN OUT THE LIGHT!

O ne of the other Gladiator aircraft commanders shared this story with us at the bar one night in the officers club. He had us all in tears of laughter!

It was not uncommon for the other branches of service to visit different officers clubs at Bien Hoa Air Force Base. Our 145th Combat Aviation Battalion was located inside the geographical boundary of the Air Force base but not near their runway or quarters.

Occasionally, they would 'slum it' and come over to the Army side of the runway for a drink. Once you got to talking to these fighter jocks, it usually wound up in some sort of swap, a ride for a ride.

On this occasion, the Gladiator aircraft commander (AC) and the fighter pilot did such a swap. A ride in an F-100 Super Sabre for a ride in one of our antiquated B-model gunships. It was agreed the Air Force pilot would get his ride first with us one morning while we were doing our routine 'flying the wire' reconnaissance around the entire Air Force base at about 0500 hrs.

As the story goes, this young captain showed up on time on the agreed morning and was quite excited. We'll call the Gladiator AC John for the sake of simplicity. Captain America (the USAF pilot) arrived at the flight line in the pitch dark, and there were handshakes all around with the crew as they were just finishing their pre-flight inspections. John walked Captain America around the aircraft, pointing out the different bits and pieces that made the helicopter differ from F-100 fighter jets.

John had made sure this young captain would be with him in the minigun ship at an altitude of about fifty feet above the jungle canopy. This would provide maximum excitement, as opposed to flying at 500 feet, approximately 200 meters behind the lower aircraft, providing cover should either of them take fire.

There was already an extra flight helmet provided at his station. Once he put it on, he looked like one of the regular guys.

Apparently, the visitor was quite enthusiastic and just about bursting with excitement. I'm sure he had never seen an M-60 machine gun with 2,000 shiny brass bullets of ammunition and had absolutely no idea of the excitement the next few hours of his life would hold. Because of the nature and hazards involved in our mission, it was agreed that the visitor would sit between the two door gunners in the back on the bench seat, not in the co-pilot's seat where the minigun site was located.

He was quite happy with that. The jet jockey was told to sit still, listen to what was being said on the intercom system, and stay out of the way if anything untoward should occur. Apparently, this was the first time his face displayed any sign of concern.

All the start procedures were engaged. The landing light was turned on, but not the position lights or the rotating beacon. This was because it worked to our advantage to remain unseen as long as possible as we performed our reconnaissance, potentially flying over some very nervous and heavily armed enemy troops. With all the radio calls made, they hovered backward out of their revetment, following through with a normal takeoff and extinguishing the landing light.

The light-fire team of two gunships took off and formed up as they climbed to 500 feet, then performed a right break, taking up a southerly course to the perimeter of the airbase. The M-60s were loaded, the circuit breakers for the minigun control and rocket launchers were pushed in, and all systems were then 'hot' for engagement. There was minimal chatter between the two gunships on their dedicated VHF radio as the short flight proceeded.

Apparently, during this part of the flight, the young captain was soaking up the atmosphere, looking around like a small bird caught in a cage, rather wide-eyed. No one in the crew was sure what he was thinking, but he looked a little unhappy.

John's call sign was Gladiator 33, while the hog ship, armed with thirty-eight rockets and two door gunners, was Gladiator 37. The airbase boundary was easy to see from the air, as it was bordered by a 200-meter-wide lightly grassed killing zone. This provided a convenient color contrast, even in the dark.

As they neared this section, the heavily fortified barbed wire boundary was easy to see as a solid black line drawn on the landscape, with an occasional machine-gun tower inside that black line.

"37, 33," came the first interchange of the day.

"Roger, 33, go ahead."

"Roger, we're commencing our descent."

"Roger, 33. Good hunting."

"33, roger that."

With that, John descended rather rapidly as they approached the jungle tree line from the cleared killing zone. Through experience, we all knew what route the wire was going to take, with the wide killing zone provided only around inhabited areas of the airfield.

It was still dark, but the ambient light from the airbase was just enough illumination to pick up the landmarks of the border itself. The biggest difficulty with performing this reconnaissance was the fact that little to nothing could be seen until the sun cracked the horizon. However, we had worked out a method of finding any troops hiding from us who would hopefully be a little trigger-happy. All we had to do was turn our landing light on and move it around like a searchlight, turn it off for about ten to fifteen seconds at a time, then turn it on again.

This method would make it nearly impossible for the bad guys to not squeeze off a few rounds when they could see exactly where we were. Then we were in business. Their muzzle flash or tracer rounds would lead straight back to their location, and that's all we needed!

John leveled off about fifty feet over the treetops and continued along the boundary. "Okay, lights coming on." With that, the two door gunners pushed out into the 80-knot slipstream of the aircraft, their M-60s at the ready, with their eyes peeled. With a flick of the landing light switch on the end of his collective, John turned on the incredibly brilliant light.

It threw a huge footprint across the jungle. Suddenly, and without warning, our brave jet jockey screamed at his highest falsetto, "What the fuck are you doing?! Turn it off! Turn it off!"

The immediate response from the crew was nothing. Their eyes were trying to penetrate the darkness, searching for any tracers that might come up in their attempt to shoot us down. John turned off the landing light when he was ready. In the meantime, the Air Force jock was rubbernecking left and right, left and right, waiting to see something arcing up toward us that was bright green and very dangerous. By now, his eyes were as big as saucers, and he was panting rapidly, obviously full of adrenaline. I'm sure the crew were wondering if he had just shat his pants!

At this point, the crew were laughing out loud, much to his embarrassment. It was explained to him in a respectful way that this was how they did business and what the expected outcomes were. He was probably also told that it had been many years since any recon aircraft had been shot down. John said that he had calmed down once he understood the tactical situation, and by the time they landed, he was chatting like a magpie and shaking hands all around as he left.

I suspect he was already planning a reciprocal ride in his F-100 for John when the time came!

26

THE UNEXPECTED END ON MY FIRST TOUR

I will take a moment to digress, cover a few explanations, and answer a few questions from those who knew me while serving with the 190th AHC regarding aircraft commander call signs.

As I mentioned before, any new pilot assigned to the 190th AHC had to serve ninety days in slicks prior to entering the gun platoon. As it turned out, I passed my aircraft commander check ride in slicks (which would usually have resulted in my permanent call sign as a Spartan), but before I was assigned a call sign for the slick platoon such as "Spartan 12," I had been assigned to the gun platoon. This meant I missed out on a permanent call sign that would follow me for the rest of my life when talking about my service as a slick pilot in the 190th.

Upon entering the Gladiator gun platoon, the progress to aircraft commander started all over again. This was a double-edged sword, as upon my entry into this platoon, all of the Gladiator call signs, which started with a 3, were taken. This meant that even if I passed my gunship aircraft commander check ride, I would still have to use the last three digits of whichever aircraft I was flying as a call sign, such as Gladiator 936.

My big day arrived on April 29th when I attended an aircraft commanders meeting. Two of our senior aircraft commanders in the Gladiator platoon had reached their DEROS. This acronym stands for Date Estimated Return From Overseas. In other words, they would leave for 'the world,' as we called it, and would not be flying in Vietnam again. This meant that two call signs were available for those of us who were already deemed aircraft commanders in the platoon.

The meeting was very upbeat, and I was assigned the UH1-B minigun aircraft with the last three serial numbers of 936. The permanent crew chief, Brian McMahon, came with the aircraft. He was a great crew chief all around. My call sign was Gladiator 37, and I was excited as hell. After the meeting, I went to the flight line where our armory sergeant needed to boresight the rocket pods. This meant that we needed to confirm the rockets would impact at exactly the point I placed a small dot of light (pipper) within the circle of imposed light in the center of the aircraft drop-down rocket sight.

This was done by aligning the aircraft, while on the ground, as closely as possible to face a distant water tower, which we used for sighting purposes at Bien Hoa. The armorer had a scope device attached to the rocket pod and, while looking through the telescopic sight and using Allen keys, aligned the pods on either side of the aircraft with the center of the water tower, approximately 700 meters away.

After the boresight was complete, we departed on my first flight as a fully-fledged Gladiator aircraft commander. We proceeded to a small area that was designated as a free-fire zone by the US Navy next to the Dong Nai River. It was only about a twelve-minute flight.

Upon being cleared into the zone, I selected what looked like an artillery crater full of water, about the size of a bunker. The rockets flew straight and true. It was great. We then returned to the Colosseum at Bien Hoa. I duly parked the aircraft in its revetment and shut it down. Just as the blades were coming to a stop, an operations clerk approached me.

"Mr. Guay, the commanding officer (CO), wants to see you in his office ASAP."

"Thanks," I replied.

It was now midafternoon, April 29, 1970, and if I recall correctly, I hadn't seen the inside of the CO's office since I reported for duty. I went straight to his office and reported to his clerk, who disappeared into the major's office and reappeared just as quickly.

The CO said, "Please come in."

As I walked in, I noticed he was standing. To my mind, this was rather unusual.

"Mr. Guay, I have a communication here from the American Red Cross. It says your presence is required back in the US as soon as possible. I want you to pack your gear tonight. I've arranged for you to get a flight to Saigon and be out of here tomorrow evening."

I stood there gawping. My mind went blank for a moment, and I couldn't find the words to speak. I was in shock. Apparently, there was no mention of why I was to return with such urgency.

"I'm not going anywhere, sir!" I said more firmly than I should have.

"Yes, you are, and you will do exactly as I've ordered!"

I could see he really meant what he said. I won't go into detail, but let's say that the argument was loud and verbose. I was pacing back and forth, making sure my commanding officer knew that I wasn't going anywhere, that I had responsibilities to my team and wasn't about to desert them under any circumstances.

Let's just say I didn't have a leg to stand on. This request from the Red Cross was ironclad. Hell, I had never heard of such a thing. Needless to say, I lost the argument, and I was absolutely furious. However, that night, I packed my duffel bag and flew out of Saigon the following night in the cargo hold of what I thought was a US Air Force KC-135 or a similar cargo jet. Only about ten passengers were in the cargo hold, and it was a long ride over the top through Alaska.

It might be worth noting that while I was waiting to board my aircraft I was sitting opposite a US Navy officer. The rows of seats were reasonably close together, so we sat there staring at each other with nothing else to do.

He finally leaned forward and said in a low voice, "I'm a Navy Seal, and I've got a souvenir. Would you like to see it?"

Well, this intrigued me. Besides, I was extremely bored.

"Sure, let's have a look," I said, leaning forward slightly.

He smiled as he undid the necklace from behind his neck and held it up between us for me to see. It was strung with what looked like small dark-pink prune-shaped objects. He was grinning from ear to ear.

I looked him in the eye and said, "What are they?"

He leaned forward and quietly said, "They're ears, from all my kills. I killed all of them with my bare hands and souvenired an ear from each of 'em."

Well, I tell you, I was shocked and impressed at the same time. He told me a few stories about several of the ears, and my conclusion was that this guy was one hell of a warrior. Of course, it is easy to have the benefit of hindsight, but I wouldn't even want to think about what PTSD has done to him by now. It wasn't long after this we boarded the flight for what we called 'the world.

I would like to mention something that happened to me during my journey home. While we were traveling, we were ordered to wear our tropical worsted uniform. It was a smart, well-pressed khaki-colored uniform. We also had to wear our medal ribbons for our awards and decorations. I didn't know this was going to make me a target of the American public, as I had been away for quite some time. I was on the last leg of my journey, transiting from New Orleans International Airport to Gulfport, Mississippi.

While I was making my way to the domestic terminal for departure, a young lady approached me, smiling, and asked, "Have you just come back from Vietnam?"

"Yes, and I'm still in one piece!" I replied with a smile.

She then stepped into my body space, pushed her face very near mine, looked me straight in the eye, and said, "Baby killer."

I felt like I had been shot in the head. I was absolutely stunned and flummoxed and just stood there with my mouth wide open. Within a few seconds, she turned on her heel and walked away to join a small gaggle of fellow idiots, all staring at me while talking among themselves and giggling.

I tried calling out after her and saying that I was in a very professional unit, and we only dealt with the enemy. Of course, that would have been to no avail anyway. I still have very hostile feelings toward her; she completely shattered my psyche.

To this day, telling that story still makes me choke up. I just can't let it go. I will never forget or forgive that woman as long as I live.

27

FINALLY, AN EXPLANATION

During this entire journey, I was still in the dark regarding the reason I had been extracted from a war zone and returned to my family. What force on earth could be powerful enough to remove a person from a theater of war against his will?

As it turns out, the sleeping giant with this enormity of power was the American Red Cross. Totally unbeknownst to me, my wife had been admitted to a mental care facility in Hattiesburg, Mississippi. To digress, she had been diagnosed as a paranoid schizophrenic approximately one year prior to my shipping out to Vietnam.

Now, she was undergoing a regimen of electric shock treatment as part of her therapy, and the appropriate medical professionals had deemed that my presence would enhance the speed of her recovery.

So, as it turns out, the Red Cross, which participated in the repatriation of wounded soldiers, also had tremendous sway when it came to having soldiers returned from the battlefields to help with the recovery of their family members. Because of the seriousness of my wife's condition, I was encouraged to request a compassionate reassignment and not to return to the war.

I will tell you that I wanted to get back to my unit more than anything on earth. I felt I was letting my comrades down. I had tasted and felt the excitement of all the elements of warfare and had developed a sense of brotherhood that only those in combat could or would understand. The overwhelming feeling of camaraderie will always remain.

I felt as if I were witnessing my best friend being beaten to a pulp and just slowly turning and walking away. I had a sense of allegiance and dedication that was being trampled upon by those who took control of my life, even if it was for what they considered a 'noble cause.' My inner self said, "Bullshit," to this entire scenario.

I knew what my brothers-in-arms were risking every day on a regular basis. They had all 'signed the check' for their lives to their country. My wife was in a hospital, with clean sheets and a safe environment, with no risks involved whatsoever. My brain was still in combat mode, and I wanted to be with those that were risking their all for their country. It was the right thing to do.

However, reality reached up and smacked me in the face. I was made to know I was also obliged to honor my allegiance to those in my personal life.

With only ninety-odd days left of my tour to serve in a theater of war, I applied for a compassionate reassignment and was transferred to Fort Rucker, Alabama.

However, the one thing I did was to pledge to myself that I would return to the Vietnam War and volunteer for a second tour.

That is exactly what I did, and I returned in June of 1972. I walked into the pages of history and became part of a team of six cross-trained pilot/gunners, who, for the first time in US Army history, were combat testing the helicopter-mounted Tubular-launched Optically-tracked Wire-guided (TOW) anti-armor missile. The First Air TOW Detachment, First Aviation Brigade. Believe me, that was a buzz!

ABOUT THE AUTHOR

Richard was born in Biloxi, Mississippi, into a US Air Force military family. After World War II, the average posting was two years at each location. While growing up, he lived in Bermuda; Fairbanks, Alaska; Ajo, Arizona; and Panama City, Florida; finally settling in Van Cleave, Mississippi, where he completed his high school education. He then studied biology and botany at Perkinston Junior College in Wiggins, Mississippi, for two years. Afterward, he joined the Sons of Tyme rock band before entering the US Army.

His draft physical in late November 1968 was the catalyst necessary to encourage him to enlist in the military. After passing his draft physical and discovering it was impossible to enter a military pilot training program without a university degree, he discovered that the US Army would accept candidates for helicopter training with the academic qualification of a high school diploma. With that, plus an additional two years of college, his academic qualifications were met. He graduated from the Warrant Officer Flight Training Program in July 1969. In 1973, he resigned his commission and became a civilian again, moved to Australia, and married a civilian Australian nurse he met on his second tour in Bien Hoa, Vietnam.

After working in a family business for twenty years, he returned to flying helicopters and working in the airline business for over thirty years, mostly in Papua New Guinea. He will be writing another book about his second tour in the Vietnam War, as well as another two books on his time flying helicopters in Papua New Guinea.

APPENDIX

ANATOMY OF THE UH-1B HELICOPTER

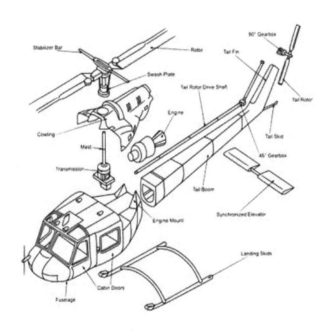

Diagram of major helicopter parts, unable to credit the original source, cannot locate on the internet.

CONTROLS

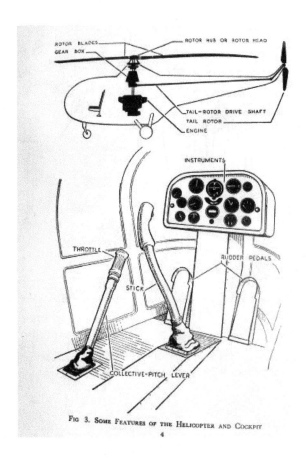

FIG 3. SOME FEATURES OF THE HELICOPTER AND COCKPIT
4

*Image used with permission of the publisher, davidandcharles.
com. Note: the 'stick' is the cyclic control, and the 'rudder pedals'
are the tail rotor control pedals or anti-torque pedals.*

COLLECTIVE CONTROL

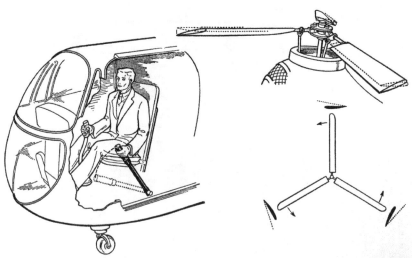

FIG. 16. PULLING THE COLLECTIVE-PITCH LEVER UP WILL INCREASE BLADE PITCH EQUALLY
ON ALL THE BLADES

Page 17, Pulling Collective Pitch
Reprinted With Permission of davidandcharles.com

PITCH CHANGE EQUALS POWER CHANGES (THROTTLE) EQUALS TORQUE CHANGE

THE HELICOPTER IN VERTICAL POWERED FLIGHT   19

The Twist-grip Throttle

To vary the speed of the rotor, the pilot must have control over the engine speed, and the normal type of throttle is the "twist-grip" type which is mounted on the end of the collective-pitch lever.

FIG. 18. THE TWIST-GRIP THROTTLE

Automatic Throttle Changes

For large alterations of blade pitch, big changes of throttle opening are necessary to maintain a given rotor speed because of the variations in blade drag. In order to take some of the work from the pilot, a simple device is fitted to the collective-pitch control system. When collective pitch is increased, a system of levers automatically opens the throttle (or appropriate method of increasing the fuel mixture to the engine) in the carburettor, and closes it as necessary when the collective-pitch lever is pushed down, the position of the throttle control in the pilot's hand not being affected. With good adjustment of this device, which is generally in the form of a cam, the pilot is relieved of much concentration, although some adjustment of the hand control is often necessary in any change of flight condition in order to keep constant r.p.m.

Page 19, Twist Grip Throttle, used with permission, davidandcharles.com.

DEFINITION OF TORQUE

MOVEMENT ABOUT THE NORMAL AXIS AND THE EFFECT OF THE TAIL ROTOR

THE normal axis of an aircraft is a straight line which passes vertically through the centre of gravity when the aircraft is in the rigging position.

TORQUE BALANCE AND DIRECTIONAL CONTROL

Now "to every action there is an equal and opposite reaction" (Newton's Third Law), so in a helicopter, when the engine

FIG. 44. TORQUE REACTION

rotates the main rotor, there is a tendency for the fuselage to be turned in the opposite direction. This is called *torque* reaction (Fig. 44).

The same thing is found in the propeller-driven aeroplane, where the tendency is for the fuselage to be rotated in the rolling plane in the opposite direction to the propeller.

Page 47, Torque Reaction, reprinted with permission of davidandcharles.com.

Balancing Torque

Some means must be used to prevent the helicopter fuselage being turned. One of the most common ways of balancing torque is by use of a tail rotor, which by exerting a side thrust on a tail arm can be made to balance the torque and prevent the fuselage turning (Fig. 45). Note that, according to which side of the tail it is mounted and the direction of its thrust when balancing torque, the tail rotor will be either a "pusher" or a "puller".

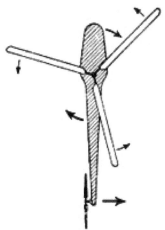

FIG. 45. BALANCING TORQUE BY MEANS OF A TAIL ROTOR

THE TAIL ROTOR. The tail rotor is driven by a take-off drive from the main-rotor gear-box and will always rotate when the main rotor is rotating. Rudder control is therefore always available in engine-off flight (in engine-off flight a free wheel fitted between the engine and gear-box automatically disconnects the engine from the rotors). The pilot can alter the collective pitch of the tail-rotor blades by using his rudder pedals. He cannot, however, control the r.p.m. of the tail rotor separately from the main rotor, and there is no mechanical cyclic-pitch change of the tail-rotor blades.

Hovering Turns

In the hovering condition, if the pilot wishes to turn the aircraft to the right (Fig. 46) he pushes on the right rudder

Page 48, Balancing torque with Tail Rotor, reprinted with permission of davidandcharles.com.

pedal. If we assume that the main-rotor blades rotate anti-clockwise when viewed from above, then the pitch of the tail-rotor blades, and therefore the thrust of the tail rotor, will be decreased and the fuselage will be turned by the difference between tail-rotor thrust and main-rotor torque (unless the pedal is pushed to the limit, in which case the blades go into negative pitch and create a thrust in the same direction as the main-rotor torque). On applying this right rudder, tail-rotor

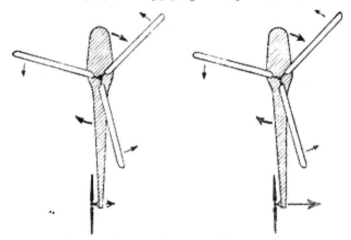

FIG. 46. TURNING RIGHT AND TURNING LEFT

thrust is reduced. The tail rotor then requires less power and the surplus will be absorbed by the main rotor. The r.p.m. of the main rotor will then rise, and unless the throttle is closed slightly the helicopter will tend to climb.

If the pilot applies left rudder, the tail-rotor thrust, which is used to balance the torque, is increased and the tail rotor will pull (or push, depending on which side of the fuselage the tail rotor is situated) the tail round to the right. Since the tail rotor needs extra power to do this, the normal r.p.m. of the main rotor will be reduced, and the helicopter will sink unless the pilot opens the throttle slightly.

Movement About the Normal Asix
Reprinted With Permission of <u>*davidandcharles.com*</u>

THE HELICOPTER IN POWERED
TRANSLATIONAL FLIGHT

THE THEORY

THE propeller-driven fixed-wing aircraft moves forward by pushing the air backwards with its propeller, the equal and opposite reaction forcing the aircraft forwards. The true

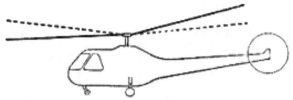

FIG. 21. ROTOR TILTED FOR FORWARD FLIGHT

helicopter has no separate propeller to provide forward propulsion. It does move forward by pushing the air backwards, however, and this is carried out by forward tilt of the rotor disc from the horizontal (Fig. 21). (The imaginary surface swept by the rotor blades during their rotation is often referred to as a disc.)

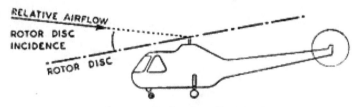

FIG. 22A. ROTOR DISC INCIDENCE

Tilting the Lift Vector

Notice that although the rotor disc may be tilted in relation to the fuselage, the drive shaft does not tilt except with changes

24

THE HELICOPTER IN POWERED TRANSLATIONAL FLIGHT 25

of fuselage attitude. The angle between the relative airflow and the rotor disc is called *rotor disc incidence* (Fig. 22A) and the

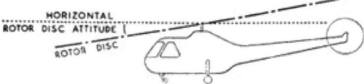

FIG. 22B. ROTOR DISC ATTITUDE

angle between the rotor disc and the horizontal is called *rotor disc attitude* (Fig. 22B). When the rotor disc is tilted, the airflow is not only down through the rotor, but slightly backwards as well. If we now examine the lift vector, we find that

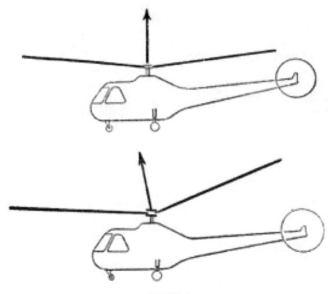

FIG. 23

instead of being vertical as it was for hovering flight it has been inclined forward slightly (Fig. 23).

Image, page 25, Helicopter in powered translational flight used with the permission of davidandcharles.com.

Movement in any Direction

During flight, a fixed-wing aircraft banks in the required direction when a turn is carried out. The lift on the wings, in addition to supplying a sustaining force holding the aircraft in the air, supplies a component towards the centre of the turn. In exactly the same way a helicopter must bank when making a turn in forward flight.

A helicopter can move in any horizontal direction while maintaining a fixed heading, merely by tilting the rotor disc in the required direction. We have seen already that the helicopter can move vertically upwards and downwards, so by combining horizontal and vertical motions we can make our helicopter move, as has so often been said, in 362 directions—all the points of the compass and up and down as well.

Fuselage Attitude

A point to note is the varying attitude of the fuselage as the helicopter accelerates forward from the hovering position.

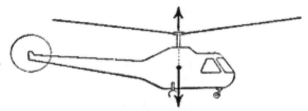

FIG. 27A. FUSELAGE ATTITUDE WHEN HOVERING

Assuming that the fuselage is level during hovering flight and that the thrust line of the main rotor passes through the c.g. of the helicopter (Fig. 27A), then when the rotor disc is tilted forward, the nose will move down owing to the forward component of the rotor thrust causing a moment about the c.g. (Fig. 27B).

This nose-down attitude will increase until the thrust line is again through the c.g. (Fig. 27c). This will occur when the forward inclination of the disc is decreased slightly.

Drag acting on the nose of the helicopter and the (normally) horizontal surfaces of the tail will also have some influence on the fuselage attitude in forward flight.

Second page Powered Translational Flight, with permission of davidandcharles.com

Author Richard Guay, ANZAC Day, April 25, 2021.
Photo by Brendan Radke/Newspix.

QR CODE LIBRARY OF CONGRESS DOCUMENTARY

URL: https://www.youtube.com/watch?v=GV1vvwdJSbc